PLANNING PROJECTS

PLANNING PROJECTS

20 Steps to Effective Project Planning

Trevor L. Young

The Industrial Society

First published in 1993 by
The Industrial Society
Robert Hyde House
48 Bryanston Square
London W1H 7LN
Telephone: 071-262 2401

ISBN 0 85290 879 2

British Library Cataloguing-in-Publication Data.
A catalogue record for this book is available from the
British Library.

Typeset by: The Midlands Book Typesetting Company
Printed by: Bourne Press
Cover design: Pylon

Text illustrations: Sophie Grillet

Reprinted 1993

Contents

List of Figures

The 20 Steps to Effective Planning

Introduction

You have just come from a meeting with your Divisional Director where you were told you have been selected to head a special project on which much of the future prosperity of the business will depend. Your emotions during this discussion varied from flattery, pride, anxiety, fear, to final euphoria as the confidence placed in you became clearer. Now, back at your desk, you start to think over the things that were said to you and the enormity of the task facing you starts to dawn. You have never done this sort of thing before and yet have sufficient self-confidence to believe that you can rise to the challenge. You have no real idea where to start and you try hard to convince yourself that after all it is only a matter of common sense.

"After all," you tell yourself, "I have had a good career with the company so far and if I succeed at this I am certain to be seriously considered for some further advancement."

Having convinced yourself that your motivational driving force is at a high level, your thoughts wander back to the primary problem facing you – where to start. On the desk in front of you is the feasibility report prepared five months ago by external consultants. You were asked to read this and report to your director in one week's time with an approach worked out. Suddenly, the telephone loudly interrupts your thoughts and brings you back to the harsh reality of day-to-day operational problems – a query as to whether you are coming to the monthly sales liaison meeting. With a sudden but short feeling of horror a glance at the wall clock tells you that the meeting started eight minutes ago. Your reputation for being well organised has taken a knock, which annoys you and you curse silently for allowing it to happen. You file the report and stride off down the corridor to the meeting, thinking as you go that you must do something about these meetings and many others. You cannot run a project and do all your other work as well. Come to think of it, that was not discussed this morning, and your feelings of anxiety return. "Can I do both at once?" you think. "Of course not," you say to yourself." That would not be expected – or would it?"

You reach the meeting room still in a state of some preoccupation and have to force yourself to concentrate on the matters in hand. After some two hours you finally escape back to the solitude of your office and your thoughts return to the earlier preoccupations. As you analyse your situation you realise that you must pass on some of your work to your small team which you feel is already in danger of being overloaded. With some careful negotiation you believe you can do this while you retain the general authority. This makes you feel more comfortable and you pick out the report, putting it in your case to take home so that you can start reading it later that evening.

Is this a familiar story to you? Have you received a project in a similar way? Were you unable to say "No" because of the attraction of a potential high-profile reward in the eyes of the senior management and your peer group? It is a frequent experience, so you are not alone in the apparent wilderness of project management.

This book is written for you, to help you enter the unknown territory of planning a project to achieve success, particularly if you have not done it before. If you have, and used trial and error and inspired judgement which worked after a fashion, perhaps you will still learn something from the contents. And if you consider yourself an expert then read on all the same – you may discover that a revision review will give you a few new ideas to try.

Why Plan?

Do you accept that we live in a world of change? "Of course we do" you say because it is obvious to everyone that things continue to change. Time moves on inexorably and with it there is a continuous movement of everything around you. The seasons come and go but they are never quite the same. Each one is unique and different in some way from the one last year. So it is with the business environment which always seems, to every generation, to be subject to more change than ever before! What is more certain is that the pace of change is increasing and promises to continue in the foreseeable future.

Technological advances affect everyone both at home and at work. If you are to survive in this climate you have to accept that the change concept is good and learn to use it rather than fight against it. You need to determine what change means for you, how you will be affected and how you can respond to manage change effectively, rather than let it manage you.

At work, change is often a subtle, accumulative process which generates new work practices or habits and becomes accepted in normal day-to-day operating activities. However, major change can create a significant disturbance to this feeling of normality and cause adverse reactions in people. Such changes are sometimes inevitable and it is only the pro-active management of the change process which can minimise reactions and their consequences to make a contribution to your organisation's future success. If you are to be effective in this pro-active mode you need to determine *in advance* the strategy and tactics of introducing a major change. This is why you must plan, to avoid difficulties or at least attempt to reduce them to a controllable level.

The process of change frequently calls for skills and knowledge which do not currently exist in your organisation. When you are faced with the challenge of making changes you have to find these skills and use them appropriately to achieve some desired results. The process of **Project Management** offers you a dynamic way to control change effectively in a structured manner. To achieve these desired results requires you to determine what needs to be done, by whom and by when, before you attempt to start the work. This is the planning process at work which allows you to prepare for change before it actually happens. Furthermore, it allows you to prepare everyone for the change through gradual development as the plan is implemented in stages to achieve the final result.

So planning is a valuable process and one with which you are already familiar. After all you would not expect to take a holiday without some preparation – getting passports, foreign currency, flight tickets and appropriate clothing. Try taking an instant holiday without this preparation and you will soon appreciate the risks you are accepting! In fact you really do very little without some planning and decision making about what you are going to do, when and how. Therefore planning has a purpose – to prepare for an enabling process that can lead to a desired result.

Planning and projects

Planning in a project environment can be described as the function of establishing a predetermined course of action, including policies and procedures, to reach some specific corporate objectives. The planning process involves you in making and taking decisions. You must first gather sufficient information to develop alternatives and then decide which to adopt before finally including this selection in the plan. In project management, planning is carried out to:

- Reduce risks and uncertainty to a minimum
- Ensure a clear understanding of the objectives
- Establish adequate standards of performance
- Provide a structured basis for carrying out the work
- Derive procedures to control the work effectively
- Obtain the optimum result with minimum effort in minimum time

Project planning is clearly operational and you are obliged to conform as closely as possible to organisational policies. Organisational procedures, however, are designed for normal day-to-day operational activities that are commonly repetitive and regular. This is not necessarily true for your project and procedures can vary from project to project according to the needs of each one. To implement the project effectively you must design these procedures, normally towards the end of the planning phase, within the broad framework of organisational procedures. But you should not be constrained by the latter. The main components of all planning are:

- Establishing the desired results – the objectives
- Determining the strategy to be followed to achieve or exceed results
- Deriving a plan and schedule showing when results are to be achieved
- A budget to establish expenditure to achieve the results
- Projections of what will happen at certain specific points in time
- Organisational structure and policies for empowerment
- Establishing procedures for control and communication
- Setting standards of performance and methods of measurement

Clearly any attempt to initiate and implement a project without these components is risking corporate disaster. Yet in many organisations managers still resist accepting the need for careful planning of a project. It is commonly believed that it is a management function that you "do as you go along" the road to the end result. The consequence of this short-sighted approach to planning could lead to:

- Wild enthusiasm
- Disillusionment
- Chaos
- Search for the guilty
- Punishment of the innocent
- Promotion of the non-participants

Certainly the planning process is dynamic and continuous. You will still be planning some of the finer points of detail of the last part of the project even during the run-down stage. However, it is essential to give an adequate amount of time to planning as a clearly recognised phase of the project at the outset. This will save much time and conflict later and avoid expensive re-work and demotivation of yourself and your team.

Summary

- *Planning is about being pro-active*
- *Planning is a dynamic process, always subject to change itself, to meet changing needs*
- *Project planning is the function of establishing a course of action in advance, to achieve some clearly specified objectives*
- *Project planning must include detailed procedures to allow effective control from start to finish*

2

Planning – the Start Point

"It's obvious where to start," you say to yourself. "You start at the beginning." Do you really? You now have in front of you that feasibility report which is the basis for the project. Your first step is to go back over this report in detail and start asking some questions about the content, such as:

- Are the assumptions made still valid?
- Is the data used still valid and completely true?
- Has any relevant data been excluded?
- Are the options and alternatives developed still the best?
- Are the costs presented up-to-date and comprehensive?
- Are the effects on current operations comprehensively assessed?
- Are the conclusions still valid?
- Are the recommendations correct now?

You read the report more than once and then decide that you need to do some checking for yourself to ensure that the answers to these questions do not uncover additional information. If they do then you must take this additional updated information into account from the start. You will almost certainly meet similar problems as the project proceeds, so it is rather important to start from several steps backwards in order to take the right steps forward.

> ## STEP 1:
> Verify the assumptions, facts, conclusions and recommendations of the Feasibility Report. Gather as much background information as possible at this stage.

So **Step 1** of planning is to verify the feasibility report, if one exists. If there is no report as the project basis there may be some other documentation which attempts to set out the scope of the project and this will need examining in detail in much the same way. You can then move on to derive clear statements which describe your role in the project. This is essential to avoid any confusion in other people's minds about what you are doing and why. It also helps you to clarify for yourself the essential elements of the role when you come to handling functional interface problems later in the project.

Your terms of reference

As project leader your role has three dimensions:

- Managing all those with an interest in the project – the stakeholders

- Managing the process – the project life-cycle
- Managing performance

To manage performance effectively requires you to manage your own from the outset. No-one's performance can be measured or evaluated unless the individual has a clear understanding of what is expected of them, the conditions under which they are expected to operate and their position in the structure. There is no-one for whom this is more important than yourself as the project leader, so before you do anything else you must set about establishing:

- Your job description for the project
- Your authority and accountability

This is often the step that is conveniently ignored by senior management who may assume that you know what is expected and leave authority undefined – sometimes on purpose! Surely if you are to achieve success you will need to know where you stand at all times and this can only be decided if you have a clear understanding of these issues. To describe your role fully, you must also ensure that you can identify two other key individuals and ensure that their roles are clearly defined:

- The project sponsor
- The accountable executive

It is possible that both roles are fulfilled by the same person but the essential point is that you have the role(s) defined.

The **Project Sponsor** is the key stakeholder who has overall responsibility for ensuring that the project meets the expectations of all stakeholders. In addition, it is this person who must ensure that the project objectives are compatible with the organisation's strategy and longer-term objectives. This person is usually highly placed in the organisation hierarchy to demonstrate the continuing support and commitment to you for the project. The sponsor is therefore in a position to influence others when resource or other problems become intractable and to give input to you on strategic issues. An awareness of other activities continuing within the broader framework of the organisation is a valuable input to you as the project proceeds.

The **Accountable Executive** is the person appointed to account to the Sponsor for the success of the project and delivery of the planned benefits contained in the project objectives. The position is normally filled by the most senior manager who has an *active interest* in the project. It is not a full- time role and the person may be

accountable for several projects at any particular time. The role is essentially to maintain close enough contact with you as project leader to ensure that the project is carefully planned and executed to defined standards. This person does not get involved in the day-to-day operational activities of the project unless you require assistance by demand. The Accountable Executive is responsible for ensuring that the project objectives are clearly defined and realistic and that the project remains viable throughout the life-cycle. Other responsibilities include a monitoring-type role on your activities for:

- The project plan and schedules
- The project budget
- Establishing success criteria
- Resolving resource conflicts at operational level
- Approvals of plans, budgets and status reports – the "sign-offs"
- Ensuring the project stays on track

If you take the analogy of the orchestra, you are the leader, the Accountable Executive is the Conductor and the Sponsor is the Director of Music.

The Accountable Executive is therefore the principal point of authority after yourself. The Sponsor will only become involved in major issues needing decisions where there are wider implications outside the project itself, ie the decisions beyond the authority delegated to the Accountable Executive.

The Accountable Executive is the person who has the responsibility for agreeing and approving your respon-sibilities for the project, usually in the form of a **Project Job Description**. Apart from setting out your responsibilities this document indicates the structural relationships you have with other managers at all levels during the life of the project.

It is imperative that during the process of establishing this document, you get a clear statement of your limits of authority and accountability. The importance of this document cannot be stressed highly enough and is a key element of your future success. The authority you are given is normally project-limited, but must be derived together with the Accountable Executive and agreed as sufficient to enable you to carry out your responsibilities effectively.

This **statement of authority** must also be published so that all functional and senior managers are aware of your role and the authority you have been given for the project. You are going to make requests on these people for support in the future, to establish priorities and negotiate for resources. Limited authority will restrict your effectiveness and put an additional burden on the Accountable Executive and the Sponsor in getting involved in resolving day-to-day operating problems.

The format for such statements varies from organisation to organisation, with formal and informal methods of communication. A typical example is given in Fig. 2.1. Generally it is preferable for you to get the facts put down in writing. If for some reason your Sponsor will not do this, then do it yourself. Prepare a simple, accurate statement setting out clearly what you understand is your position in the structure and the limits of your authority specifically in your role as project leader. Then present this document for agreement and approval! At least it will provoke senior management into realising that you intend to manage your project in an organised manner and force them to face up to some delegation as a matter of clear necessity.

MEMORANDUM
from the

MANAGING DIRECTOR'S OFFICE

TO: Terry Downs
Date: 1 July 1991

Subject: Project SCOR - New Premises for Sales & Admin. Depts.

Further to our conversation yesterday I confirm the main points of our discussion.

1. The role of Project Sponsor will be fulfilled by myself
2. The Accountable Executive for this project will be Graham Watson. The responsibilities and authority of this role are set out in a separate note to Graham, a copy of which is attached for your records.
3. You are appointed Project Leader for the complete duration of the project through to successful handover of the new premises to the House Services Manager.
4. In your role as Project Leader you are accountable to Graham Watson for all aspects of the project and it's timely, successful completion.
   You are fully aware of the consequences of late occupation on our new business structure for 1992.
5. Your authority for the purposes of the project is limited as follows:

All purchasing decisions for capital equipment must be counter signed by Colin Appleby. All revenue commitments over five thousand pounds total value on any order must be similarly countersigned.

Normal Company Standing Instructions Apply to the raising and preparation of purchase documentation. You have full authority to acquire the resources you need at any time by direct discussion with line managers to agree who is released to you, for what time period and the priorities of that individual's workload. If the skills you require are not readily available you may seek these externally as temporary resource inputs provided this does not adversely affect the budget.

You have complete authority as an officer of the Company in all dealings with the Local Authorities and our appointed consultants and suppliers. Your decisions will be firm and final subject to normal management controls with Graham and myself.

I would like you to initially discuss and agree your job description for the project with Graham and start the project planning process. All line managers will be informed of your appointment to this project at the Briefing next Thursday, when I will stress the importance of their support and co-operation with the project team.

I would appreciate you confirming receipt and acceptance of this note and it's contents.

   Thank you

Fig. 2.1   Get a statement of authority and accountability

Your responsibilities

You are going to manage the project on a day-to-day operational basis, apart from carrying out the duties of your normal line function either as a member of a functional team or a manager. You obviously need to have a clear understanding of what additional responsibilities are being loaded on to you for the project. These responsibilities include:

- Establish clear objectives, approved by the key stakeholders
- Agree approval procedures with the stakeholders
- Prepare all project plans and get them approved
- Establish the project control system and measurement criteria
- Establish the project budget
- Ensure all project activities are carefully monitored
- Track project progress and produce regular status reports
- Resolve all conflicts promptly
- Maintain regular contact with stakeholders
- Manage the project team
- Monitor performance at all levels
- Ensure problems are promptly identified and corrective action taken
- Make or force required decisions at all levels to achieve objectives
- Deliver the expected outcomes at each stage, on time, on budget

This is not a comprehensive list and other items may be included according to the type of work involved or organisational needs. In preparing your own job description, you must attempt to determine the duties you expect to carry out in the interests of the project to achieve success – not those which merely lead to your self-gratification! However, it is not enough just to identify the list of responsibilities. You must then insert these in summary form into a statement of the job description. This can be formalised if your organisation has a standard format. If one does not exist, now is the time to introduce the concept both for yourself and for your project team.

Through deriving the Project Job Description and statement of authority you can clearly define who approves the work of the project. At certain key points in the process of developing plans and executing the work it is essential to get the results accepted and approved or "**signed off**". This process is essential in project work to minimise re-work and indecision, to maintain momentum with commitment at all levels, and to keep a clear sense of direction.

> *STEP 2:*
> *Identify the Sponsor and Accountable Executive*
> *Establish your Project Job Description*
> *Identify your Key results Areas*
> *Get a clear statement of Authority & Accountability*

Key result areas

Although the job description is designed to identify the principal duties of the job it is helpful to focus these more accurately by identifying the **Key Result Areas** for the job. As a guide, you can derive these KRAs from the four process management aspects of the role:

- Planning
- Organising

- Directing
- Controlling

Each of these processes contains specific results that you need to achieve if the project is to reach a successful conclusion. A typical list of activities for the KRAs is given in Fig. 2.2.

Key Results Areas are the parts of the job where you are expected to get results, which means that performance in these areas must be measurable in some way. This helps you as well as the Sponsor to identify very clearly where performance is adequate, or more or less than adequate, as the project proceeds. Such inputs are valuable to you as part of your own personal development and you must apply the same principles to your team members.

```
┌─────────────────────────────────────────────────────────────┐
│                                                               │
│           KEY RESULT AREAS - PROJECT LEADER                   │
│                                                               │
│   PLANNING                                                    │
│                                                               │
│       Derive the project plans for execution and control     │
│       Derive the project schedules                            │
│       Prepare the project budget and cost control procedures  │
│       Derive the project procedures for monitoring and tracking│
│       Design the project control system and action planning procedures│
│       Modify plans as required to meet project objectives     │
│       Agree and approve all project specifications and standards│
│                                                               │
│   ORGANISING                                                  │
│                                                               │
│       Derive the project organisation structure chart         │
│       Prepare project team member's job descriptions          │
│       Select team members with appropriate skills             │
│       Identify individual responsibilities                    │
│       Identify and communicate project priorities             │
│       Maintain continuous review of resource needs to meet objectives│
│                                                               │
│   DIRECTING                                                   │
│                                                               │
│       Establish a system for problem solving                  │
│       Establish procedures for decision taking within the team│
│       Provide all team members with opportunities for personal development│
│       Derive personal performance targets for all team members│
│       Maintain a continuous monitoring of team morale         │
│       Act promptly to deal with inter and intra-team conflicts│
│       Maintain close contact with stakeholders                │
│                                                               │
│   CONTROLLING                                                 │
│                                                               │
│       Monitor all project activities to ensure they are objective directed│
│       Carefully monitor for conformity to plans, specifications and standards│
│       Evaluate actively and learn from successes and mistakes │
│       Hold regular progress reviews with relevant personnel   │
│       Issue project status reports at planned intervals       │
│       Ensure all procedures and systems are utilised effectively│
│       Promote harmonious working relationships with all functional areas│
│                                                               │
└─────────────────────────────────────────────────────────────┘
```

Fig. 2.2   The project leader's Key Result Areas

Summary

- *Vertify the Feasibility Report*
- *Establish the Project Structure in the organisation structure*
- *Identify the Key Stakeholders, their role and responsibilities*
- *Establish your Project Job Description and Key Results Areas*
- *Establish your Authority and Accountability in writing*

Preparations for Planning

Having established your terms of reference with your job description and a statement of authority and accountability you can complete the preparations for the planning process. Your project has four clear phases which comprise the **Project Life-cycle**:

- Conception
- Planning
- Implementation and execution
- Run-down and termination

Steps 1 and 2 are essentially preparation for planning and are integral to the conception phase of the project. Before you can start planning in earnest you must ensure that you have a clearly defined set of project objectives. Too many projects are perceived to fail because of the lack of clear objectives. This step must not be bypassed with excuses about difficulty or inability at this point in time to finalise the results which the organisation needs to achieve.

Poor or lack of objectives is a symptom of weak management with no clear sense of direction or strategy. In order to derive clear objectives effectively it is necessary to establish the project results that the organisation is seeking within the broader context of corporate strategy and longer-term objectives. This provides you with signposts to corporate priorities and at the same time will probably yield some information to you about the constraints the organisation faces in the months ahead. Such information may have a serious effect on your project at some point in the future and the more advance data you can collect, the better you can plan actions to take as contingencies if the need does arise.

STEP 3:

Identify the project objectives:
The problem or need as perceived
The purpose of the project
The benefits to the organisation of deriving a solution
Definition of the results to be achieved
The deadlines for the results to be achieved
Get the Objectives Statement signed off as approved

Setting project objectives is never easy to do, but easy to avoid. The most common avoidance technique you face is the excuse that: "We are not quite sure yet where this project is going to end." Of course no-one can predict the future, but a more positive approach is to work to achieve results that the organisation needs to help meet the corporate objectives. Some guidelines for setting the project objectives are given in Appendix One. The suggested approach will help you arrive at the initial **objectives statement**, which is the foundation of all planning. This process does not exclude the possibility that the statement may change later, even during planning, but the key elements of the objectives statement can then be maintained and modified as stakeholder expectations change.

Assemble the project team

Before you start planning you must start to assemble the team. How you go about this process depends on the project size and complexity. There are many options available, but resource constraints may exist to limit the way you can structure the team. Your team could comprise:

- Yourself alone
- Yourself plus one or more dedicated team members to form a core team
- Yourself plus part-time members from your own line functional area and other functional areas
- Yourself plus representatives from other functional areas
- Yourself plus a permutation of the above

If possible, identify those individuals who are going to have a high level of input to the work of the project. These are the people you select as the **Core Team Members** and, because of their later input, it is important to involve them in the actual planning process. They may come from your own functional area as subordinates, colleagues or even from a higher grade than you! Alternatively they may be **Representatives** from key functional areas whom you will make responsible for carrying out significant parts of the work of the project. The representative does not necessarily carry out the work personally, but is responsible for ensuring that the work does get done on time by the department by assigning the work to others within the department. You are not concerned with who does the work, only that it is completed according to the plan and to the standards you specify.

STEP 4:

Select appropriate team members
Hold inaugural team meeting
Explain project objectives, purpose and corporate context
Ensure understanding
Explore team experience

You start the planning process with this core team, some of whom you may have had little or no contact with previously. From now on you must start the process of building this group of individuals into a working unit – the project team. This is the time for testing your leadership ability as team dynamic processes start to operate and you must use your skills to minimise conflict and disagreements. You can effectively assist this by instituting a regular 1:1 meeting with each team member to start to learn more about them as people and understand them and their abilities better.

Your first action with the team is to hold the inaugural team meeting where you can:

- Welcome them onto the team
- Describe the project objectives
- Share your own enthusiasm and commitment to the project

- Ensure that everyone clearly understands the project objectives and the purpose of the project in terms of corporate strategy
- Explore the team's previous experience in projects or similar work
- Explain how you intend to proceed with the planning process
- Explain the basic standards you expect from the team
- Answer any relevant questions you are asked

The conception phase of the project is now essentially complete, with only one important activity left before you start the real planning of the project.

Identify the stakeholders

Now that you have assembled your team it is appropriate to identify all those groups and individuals whom you and the team believe have, or could possibly have, an interest in your project. This may be confined to the Sponsor and the Accountable Executive (the "inner" stakeholders) along with any external groups or consultants ("outer" stakeholders) who have had an involvement in the feasibility report prepared earlier. With the team, attempt to identify functional line managers who have an interest through providing resources or data inputs to the project. At this stage the list will not be complete. As you develop the project plans more stakeholders will become apparent to you, particular those external to the organisation, such as suppliers of services, materials and equipment.

> **STEP 5:**
>
> *Identify all known stakeholders*
> *Classify as Inner and Outer*
> *Determine relative importance of each*
> *Rank the list – assign responsibility for managing*
> *Review the list at regular intervals*

At some point, you need to give all stakeholders a valuation to assign the responsibility for managing each stakeholder to a team member. The list of stakeholders you derive is not constant and is always subject to change, so you must review it regularly. *Make this a regular item on the agenda of your project review meetings.*

Summary

- *Establish the project objectives*
- *Select project team, ensuring team members have appropriate skills*
- *Hold team meeting and ensure everyone understands the project purpose and objectives*
- *Start building your team identity*
- *Identify all those with an interest in your project – the stakeholders*

4

Building Your Plan

Up to this point you have carried out preparative groundwork for the real planning process to start. You have selected a core team of just a few people who are going to assist you in building the plan. The size of this team has really been decided without having a clear idea of the total amount of work involved. The full picture of resource needs for the project is not known this early in the project, so the core team is more important. It is therefore valid to stress that selection of the right skills and experience in these team members is crucial to your future success.

Clearly you cannot develop your plan until the building blocks have been established. The first of these is a complete list of all the tasks which have to be carried out throughout the project. However, everyone knows that this is not a realistic objective since that much detail is not available, particularly on a project that will take several months to complete.

The projects that have a high number of unknowns and possible options, often termed "soft" projects, have even greater problems of detail definition in the early stages.

The Objectives Statement lists the key elements of the work to be carried out through the inter-related results to be achieved. This gives the basic foundations of the project, but you now set about gathering as much additional information as possible through a fact-finding exercise by all the team. This will allow you to draw up a **scope of work** statement – a narrative statement of the work required for the project. The purpose of this document is to identify clearly what is involved in executing the project in order to achieve the objectives.

The scope of work

This document is a natural extension of the project objectives statement to describe the strategy and tactics of arriving at the desired conclusion at the end of the project. The fact-finding exercise will provide much of the data you need to derive the statement. In addition you must consult the key stakeholders and any others whom you value as important to establish a clear understanding of their needs and expectations from the project. These are not always immediately apparent. You may believe there are covert agendas in people's minds and you must try to get these into the open early in the project. Recording clear statements from stakeholders at this stage will avoid conflict later.

It is also valid to establish what role each stakeholder expects to play in the project from this point so that you can clarify their individual responsibilities and contributions. Again it is prudent to record this involvement and its limitations for future reference. Finally, you must establish if any specifications exist or are planned to be prepared by any stakeholders for the project. Ensure that these are available now, or that firm commitments are made to provide them by a specific date. These could be customer-produced or come from the end user, but you do not want to find such documents appearing after several weeks' work has been done. Your project deadlines do not allow the luxury and inefficiency of carrying out extensive re-work.

STEP 6:

Establish the SCOPE OF WORK statement
Describe the work to be executed
Clarify stakeholder's needs & expectations
Check for specifications
Get the SOW signed off as approved

As the SOW often refers to specifications it is appropriate to draw up a Project Specifications List. Specifications are normally associated with hardware or equipment and materials. Later on in the process of planning you can also draw up specifications for all project procedures if these do not already exist in the organisation. You may include specifications for:

- Project monitoring and tracking
- Project status reporting
- The control system
- Cross-function communication
- Problems – early warning system
- Project timesheet recording

Your organisation may have others, particularly in the area of financial control, which you need to incorporate in your list. It is often useful to issue the complete set of specifications as a bound book to all team members and key stakeholders. This ensures that everyone clearly understands the procedures and practices you are using at the point of project implementation and execution.

> **STEP 7:**
> Compile the SPECIFICATION BOOK
> Collect all known specifications
> Derive new ones where possible at this stage
> Include established procedures where appropriate
> Have all documents signed off as approved
> Issue the book as considered appropriate

Identifying the project tasks

You now need to start identifying all the work of the project to prepare a plan. This means literally trying to identify every task that has to be executed to complete the whole project. Except with very hard projects this is difficult at this stage and you can only hope to identify the major parts of the work, leaving some of the real detail until later.

Identification of the project tasks is a team activity – the more heads focusing past experience and knowledge on the problem and on the tasks to be executed, the more accurate the plan will turn out eventually. Use the familiar technique of *brainstorming* as a group activity to draw up a list of tasks. For guidelines on how to conduct a brainstorming session, see Appendix Two.

Use a white board or preferably a flip chart to record all the tasks you and the team can think of. Do not concern yourself in trying to group them yet, but concentrate on getting as many tasks as possible identified. Quantity rather than quality is the need at this stage. Although the list is not necessarily complete it does not matter as long as you have identified enough tasks to start grouping them together in clusters. You are looking to group together all tasks that relate closely to each other for one particular aspect of the project. Examples of this process for the sample project SCOR are shown in Fig. 4.1 – the result of the brainstorming, and Fig. 4.2 – the task list formed into clusters.

You have now established the **KEY STAGES** of the project – all the principal areas of work to be carried out to complete the project. It is likely that many tasks which form part of the detail will not have been identified yet, but you will certainly now have a much clearer picture of the main chunks of work involved. Reducing the work to the key stages has many benefits for you:

- Fewer "tasks" to manipulate in planning
- Individual stages can be readily exploded to show detail
- Convenient for status reporting to senior management
- Permits easier assignment of responsibility for execution
- Provides focus for identifying project milestones

Although you have identified all the key stages and all the team agree that you have got it right, all you really have is a list of the work to be done. There is no sequence showing the inter-relationships between the key stages and this logic must be decided by you and the team before anything else is done.

PROJECT SCOR

LOCATE SUITABLE BUILDING
LOCATION FOR ACCESS BY
STAFF
CHECK FACILITIES - CAR PARK
ETC
AVAILABILITY
CURRENT USE - PLANNING?
SERVICES AVAILABLE
CONSENTS
LEGAL ASPECTS
COST LEASE ETC
MODIFICATIONS REQUIRED
LAYOUT INSIDE
APPROVALS - LOCAL
AUTHORITY
NUMBER OF STAFF TO
ACCOMMODATE
DECISION ON OPEN PLAN?
DECISION ON CATERING IN
BLDG
FIND SUITABLE BUILDERS FOR
MODS
GET QUOTES FOR MODS
ASSESS QUOTES
DECISION ON BUILDER
DECORATORS - GET QUOTES ?

COMPLETE DECORATION INSIDE
FURNITURE NEEDS
QUOTES FOR FURNITURE
PURCHASE FURNITURE
INSTALL FURNITURE

DECIDE ON FITTINGS
QUOTES FOR FITTINGS
PURCHASE FITTINGS
INSTALL FITTINGS
DECIDE NEW STAFF NEEDED
START RECRUITMENT PROCESS
SELECT NEW STAFF
TRAIN NEW STAFF
I T SYSTEM DESIGN
COMPUTER NEEDS

COMPUTER FACILITIES
HOW MANY TERMINALS?
TELEPHONES
LINES TO OTHER OFFICES
TESTING OF I T SYSTEM
SOFTWARE NEEDS

INSTALLATION OF OTHER
EQUIPMENT
OTHER OFFICE EQUIPMENT
FAX MACHINES
INSTALLATION OF FURNITURE
TRAINING FACILITY EQUIPMENT
TESTING OF ALL EQUIPMENT
QUOTES FOR I T SYSTEM
STAFF FAMILIARISATION
QUOTES FOR ALL OTHER
EQUIPMENT   MOVE STAFF
INTO BUILDING
MOVE FILES AND OTHER
MATERIALS
FINAL TESTING OF SYSTEMS
PURCHASE OF EQUIPMENT
INFORM CUSTOMERS

GRAND OPENING
CONTACT LOCAL MP TO OPEN
BLDG
ARRANGE CATERING FOR
OPENING
INVITATIONS OUTSIDE

OTHERS
SECURITY SYSTEMS
FIRE ALARM SYSTEMS
FIRE EXTINGUISHERS
CAR PARK LAYOUT

RECEPTION FACILITY - DO WE
NEED?
INTERVIEW ROOMS ?
TRAINING ROOM?
LARGE MEETING ROOM?
UTILITY KITCHENS FOR STAFF?
WASHROOM NEEDS?

Fig. 4.1   Brainstorming the task list

PROJECT SCOR - KEY STAGES

LOCATE BUILDING
LOCATION FOR ACCESS
CHECK FACILITIES
AVAILABILITY
CURRENT USE
SERVICES AVAILABLE
LEGAL ASPECTS
COST LEASE ETC
CONSENTS

PLAN LAYOUT
NO OF STAFF
DECISION ON OPEN PLAN
DECISION ON CATERING
RECEPTION FACILITY
INTERVIEW ROOMS
MANAGERS OFFICES
TRAINING ROOM
MEETING ROOM
WASHROOM NEEDS
UTILITY KITCHENS

CLEAN UP INSIDE
CONTRACTOR
QUOTES
ORDER

MODIFICATIONS
FIND BUILDER
ARCHITECT NEEDED?
GET QUOTES
AGREE MODS REQUIRED
DECIDE BUILDER & SIGN CONTRACT
FIND SUITABLE DECORATORS
SELECT DECORATOR
SIGN CONTRACT WITH DECORATOR
AGREE DATES FOR WORK

GET APPROVALS
LOCAL AUTHORITIES
GENERAL SERVICES
INSURANCE COMPANY
TELEPHONES
OTHERS

CARRY OUT MODIFICATIONS

FITTINGS & FIXTURES
DESIGN
QUOTES, PURCHASE ORDERS
AGREE DELIVERY DATES

I T & C SYSTEMS
DESIGN SYSTEM,
QUOTES FOR SUPPLY
EQUIPMENT NEEDS
TELEPHONES, FAXES
COMPUTER FACILITIES
LINES TO OTHER OFFICES
SOFTWARE NEEDS
QUOTES FOR HARDWARE
OFFICE EQUIPMENT
TRAINING EQUIPMENT
QUOTES FOR EQUIPMENT
PURCHASE & DELIVERY DATES

NEW STAFF
DECIDE ON NUMBERS
START RECRUITMENT
SELECT & TRAIN STAFF

INSTALL FITTINGS

INSTALL OFFICE EQUIPMENT

INSTALL I T & C SYSTEM

TESTING I T & C SYSTEM & EQUIP.

MOVE STAFF AND MATERIALS

FURNITURE
DECIDE NEEDS
QUOTES AND SELECT SUPPLIER
PURCHASE ORDER & DELIVERY

INSTALL FURNITURE

FINAL TESTING OF SYSTEMS

GRAND OPENING
LOCAL DIGNITARY?
INVITATIONS & CATERING

OPEN BUILDING

Fig. 4.2   The task list grouped into Key Stages

STEP 8:
  Identify the project tasks
    Use brainstorming with ALL the core team
    Cluster together closely related tasks
    Identify the KEY STAGES of the project

Deducing the logic

It may seem obvious to suggest you must get all the key stages in their natural sequence for execution, yet this fundamental step is often omitted by project leaders. It is assumed that everyone knows what to do and the order in which things are to be done. By deducing the logic you are sure you have got it right, and it is really a very simple process. You can analyse the data just by shuffling information around on a bar chart, but this is time-consuming and expensive on pencil erasers! There is a simple technique to help you – **Taskboarding**. For this your materials are a pencil, pad of self-adhesive notelets (or 5' × 4' file cards) and, for a feeling of security, a pencil eraser.

Taskboarding – the method

Take your list of key stages and write the title of each key stage on a separate notelet or file card, ensuring you leave the bottom inch or so clear for other information later. As you prepare the notelets stick them on a whiteboard, or even the wall, in a random list. (If you are using file cards then you will need a fair-sized table cleared for this technique.) Once you have all the notelets prepared, sit down with your team and decide together which of the key stages comes first. Stick this first notelet on the wall leaving plenty of space to the right. Then decide which stage(s) starts immediately after completion of the first. Locate the relevant notelets to the right of the first notelet on the wall. Then continue to ask the basic questions:

- What can I do now that this work is completed that I could not do before?
- Upon which key stage or key stages is the next key stage dependent?
- Upon which key stages is this key stage not dependent in order to execute the work?

By continuing this process, debating as a team the relationships between the key stages you will eventually arrive at

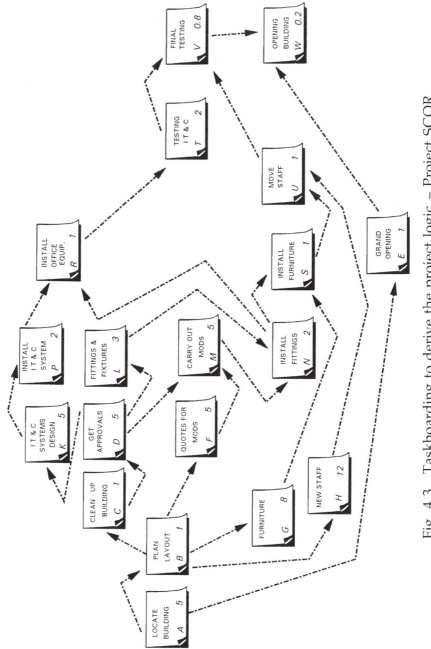

Fig. 4.3 Taskboarding to derive the project logic – Project SCOR

a complete picture of the project logic, having used up all your notelets. The result is a logic picture similar to the example shown in Fig. 4.3. It is acceptable to leave the logic arrangement on the wall for one or two days for further review and reflection. You may get other ideas and change the sequence, split key stages into more than one stage or combine stages together. The logic diagram is the foundation of your project and takes time to get it right. The arrows in the diagram indicate the flow or sequence of the **KEY STAGES** or **ACTIVITIES** of your project.

It is appropriate to label each key stage with some identification code or label working from left to right across the diagram. Having established the logic you are now closer to getting some idea of how long the project is going to take, regardless (for the time being) of the time-limit that may have been set for you.

To do this you need to insert the **DURATION** for each key stage on each notelet as shown in Fig. 4.3. The basis of the duration must be defined clearly so that a consistent approach is taken by everyone. Normally for the first attempt to plan the project it is appropriate to work with *person-days* based on *one* individual executing the work of any key stage. Alternatively you can work with *direct hours* as the unit of duration. At this stage of planning you do not need to concern yourself with the type of resource or how many people are to work on certain parts of the project. It is worth recording the logic structure as a list of **DEPENDENCIES** as shown in Fig. 4.4.

This shows clearly which key stage is dependent on other key stages right through the project. You may decide later to split some stages into two or more as the detail emerges.

Tail	Head	CODE	Description	DURATION weeks	1	2	3	4	5
		A	Locate Bldg	5	NIL				
		B	Plan layout	1	A				
		C	Clean up bldg	1	B				
		F	Quotes for mods	5	B				
		G	Furniture quotes	5	B				
		H	Recruit staff	12	B				
		D	Get all approvals	5	C				
		M	Install mods.	5	F	D			
		L	Design fittings	3	D				
		K	Design IT&C & quotes	5	D				
		P	Install IT&C	2	K				
		N	Install fittings	2	L	M			
		R	Install office equpt	1	P	N			
		S	Install furniture	1	N	G			
		T	Test IT&C equpt	2	R				
		U	Move staff	1	S				
		V	Final testing	0.8	U	T			
		W	Grand opening	0.2	V	E			
		E	Plan opening	1	A				

Fig. 4.4 Project SCOR dependency list

Unless you conclude that you have made a serious error with your logic, splitting should be minimised or avoided, as this will necessitate a full re-analysis of the plan.

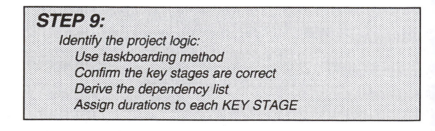

STEP 9:
Identify the project logic:
Use taskboarding method
Confirm the key stages are correct
Derive the dependency list
Assign durations to each KEY STAGE

You have now derived the basic plan with its logic carefully identified. When you are quite satisfied that this is correct, or at least as correct as it can be with the information you have available, you can start to develop the detail.

Regardless of the planning tools you might select to use from this point forward you will need to develop the key stages into a **Work Breakdown Structure** as an extension of your primary logic. This is a convenient graphic format for presentation of all the tasks that have to be carried out through the project. It is easy to understand, amend and add to as more detail becomes available later in the project. The key stages you have derived are essentially **first level planning** and the work breakdown structure is the method you use to expand the stages into second, third or more levels of detail. The appropriate level of detail you require contributes to the conclusions you derive about which planning tools you are going to use.

Summary

- *Derive the SCOPE OF WORK statement*
- *Collect all specifications together into a SPECIFICATION BOOK*
- *Use BRAINSTORMING techniques to identify as many tasks as possible at this stage*
- *Cluster the tasks into related groups to derive the KEY STAGES*
- *Use TASKBOARDING to develop the LOGIC diagram*

5

The Work Breakdown Structure

Now that you have identified the *key stages* of the project along with the corresponding logic you have derived the data for the first level planning to be completed. As the name infers, the **Work Breakdown Structure** (or **WBS** as it is commonly named) is a very convenient vehicle for deriving a complete breakdown of each of the key stages into their smaller elements. It is possibly the most important document in your project file, providing the framework for all subsequent activities you carry out to complete the project successfully. It provides the basic data for:

- The final schedule of all activities and tasks
- The basis of building a project budget
- Project budget and cost control
- Project tracking

- Status reporting procedures
- Network development
- Performance measurement
- Resource assignment and control

The major benefit of using the WBS is that you are unlikely to omit any important detail that is necessary for project success. Also it is a convenient format that is easy for non-project people to understand. It is the foundation of all planning at more than one level.

Multi-level planning

There are various models used for the WBS, with anything from one to nine levels. It is more common to have around four to six levels:

- The overall plan – the "big picture" based on the KEY STAGES
- The KEY STAGE project – treating each of the key stages as a small project in a specific time-frame
- The tasks that need to be carried out in each KEY STAGE
- The Work Packages (or PLANS) for each task assignment in each KEY STAGE

The larger the project the more likely you will have to break it down into more detail and hence more levels. Key stages may be broken down first into activities, each of which is divided into tasks and sub-tasks and even broken down again for functional execution (by different departments even on different sites). This process could add up to another four levels of planning detail to the WBS.

Developing the detail

To derive the detail for each of the key stages you may need to involve different people. If some of the work is to be the responsibility of a department, then clearly a representative of that department must be brought in to the planning activity. You can then be absolutely sure that nothing is left out, and also that the time estimates are more realistic.

It is helpful to take each key stage in turn and derive the detail using the brainstorming and taskboarding techniques used earlier. Cluster the detail in the same way to derive the second, third and, if appropriate, fourth level of detail. Finally, enter the data you derive into the WBS which is

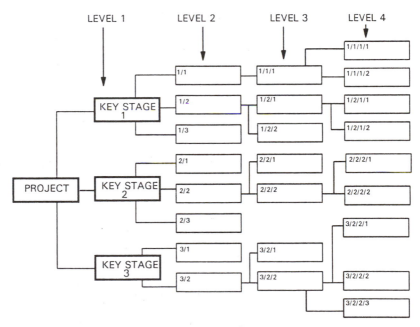

Fig. 5.1   The Work Breakdown Structure

drawn in the same way as an accountability chart (see Fig. 5.1).

When you have completed the chart based on current information, you can use this as the basis for making decisions about who does what on the project. You can expand the amount of detail you display in the WBS according to your needs. You can include the name of the resource assigned to each activity and even include start and finish times or dates. The chart does not show the logic and, although this is feasible, it might confuse the reader in practice. You know that the structure has

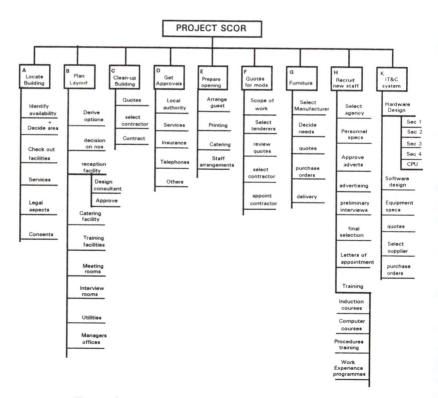

Fig. 5.2   Part of the WBS for Project SCOR

been developed based on clearly derived logic and this is not altered by expanding each key stage to show all the relevant detail. However, if you conclude that your original estimate of the time to complete a key stage is in error, then this could have a consequential effect on other key stages and affect the total project time. Part of the WBS for the sample project SCOR is developed in Fig. 5.2.

STEP 10:
Develop the Work Breakdown Structure
Start with the Key Stages as Level 1
List activities in each key stage
Use as many levels as appropriate

A consistent approach

One of the major benefits of the WBS is its ready acceptance as a display document which everyone at all levels can easily understand. It is therefore a very convenient planning tool for your organisation to use as a common fundamental approach to all project planning. Organisational synergy is developed by this consistency, and the methods used to develop the WBS can be drawn up as a checklist for all departments and Project Leaders to use.

It is also the primary document for establishing the **project operating budget** or confirming the original budget from the feasibility report. Your budget may have been approved at senior level based on this report. The WBS is used to generate the cost analysis for budget variances resulting from the detailed planning work. There can be no doubt in anyone's mind where and why the costs are estimated to be higher and this is important information in the process of decision-taking about the operating budget (see Chapter 12).

The WBS is also the fundamental document from which you draw up the project milestones – the key progress points in the project.

Setting the milestones

Every project has milestones and you have two established at the outset:

- The start date
- The finish date

Using the WBS, you can decide the most important key stages and assign their completion milestone status. Other milestones you can identify could include:

- Review meetings with key stakeholders
- Prototype ready for testing
- Certain procurements
- Testing
- Writing of literature or manuals
- Project deliverables – data outputs for a later stage
- Status reports at specific points of progress

It is worth establishing a **Milestone Schedule** now and ensure that this is acceptable to the key stakeholders as well as to the team. This document is an essential project data sheet for all those involved in the project. It allows you to keep everyone in the picture with the project objectives and how you want them achieved through the intermediate deadlines that you have "frozen" as milestones. A typical schedule is shown in Fig. 5.3.

MILESTONE SCHEDULE

PROJECT TITLE:		JOB NUMBER: *P336/191/JW*	
SCOR		Sponsor:	*J. Williams*
Project Leader:	*T R Downs*	Accountable	*G B Watson*
Date Initiated:	*January 1991*	Executive:	
START DATE: *1 - 3 - 91*		FINISH DATE: *16 - 8 - 91*	
PRIMARY MILESTONES:		Planned	Actual
Locate building & secure lease		▲	
Secure all necessary approvals			
Completion of modifications			
Installation of all I T & C equipment		▲	
Staff Moves			
Indicate MUST DATES with a ▲			
Prepared By: *FJS*	Checked By: *TRD*	Approved By: *GBW*	
Date: *20 - 2 - 91*	Date: *21 - 2 - 91*	Date: *23 - 2 - 91*	

Fig. 5.3   Statement of project milestones

STEP 11:

Derive the Milestone Schedule
Identify the milestone points
Identify which will have Must Date status
Get the schedule signed off as approved with the WBS

You will notice two things in the schedule at this point:

■ The absence of dates – you haven't matched your plan to a calendar yet

■ A new date – the *Must Date* has appeared

Dates can be inserted into the schedule at this point, although it is preferable to do this once you have confirmed all your plans and the activity durations with stakeholder approvals after the next step in planning. The *must date* is a convenient way of prioritising any particular milestone by giving it an absolute position in the plan. You are effectively saying that short of Acts of God and War the project MUST meet that obligation because of horrific downstream consequences if it does not!

Time to decide?

You are now faced with an important decision. You have the basic plan formulated and developed into the detail. That raises certain questions to be answered:

- How is the plan to be displayed for tracking progress
- Do we need to develop the plan any further for control purposes?
- Which tools do we use for further development of the plan?
- What information is needed in reporting progress and for tracking the project?

The conclusions you now draw are critical and depend on the size of the project, how many people are involved and how important the project is for the organisation. Which is the appropriate approach to use from now on is really decided upon by past experience and the amount of control you consider necessary for project success.

You may feel that a short duration project which you believe may take only a few weeks to complete does not justify a rigorous analytical approach in planning. There is a common misconception that the techniques used require detailed technical knowledge and practice. In fact you will be surprised to find that very little practice is required to

adopt these techniques for most projects. The benefits to you will soon become apparent when you come to control the project progress. This is especially valid when you are faced with executing a crash programme as a fast response to a competitive situation. Getting a new or modified product into the market-place rapidly is a potential disaster area without careful planning and, particularly, attention to the detail. This is not to demote the scope of application for simple methods of planning since they have a long history of successful use. Short projects with only a few people or even one person involved can be adequately planned and controlled with the simple method. The use of any method pays dividends in the sense that at least the project activities are planned!

Up to this point your planning process has followed a number of steps in sequence. At some of these steps you have the option to take a bypass if you do not think it is appropriate to the project at that particular point in time.

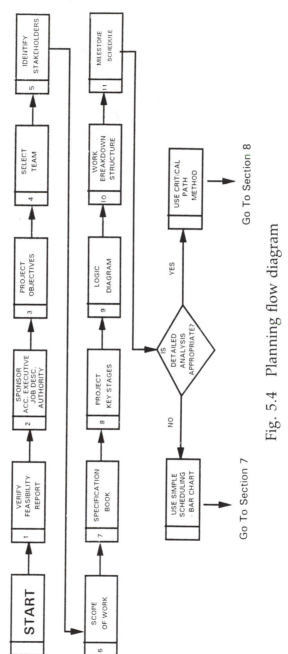

Fig. 5.4 Planning flow diagram

The steps you have taken are shown in the flow diagram in Fig. 5.4, which also shows the decision point you have reached now. As your planning proceeds, the flow diagram will be completed so as to give you a complete route map for project planning.

The options you have are therefore either:

- Use simple scheduling with a Bar Chart
  or
- Use a Critical Path Method for scheduling

Each has certain benefits and the choice you make is dependent on the size and complexity of the project. The **Critical Path Methods** have the advantage of allowing you to rigorously analyse your project logic to determine the real critical elements and the spare time available in others. This is obviously valuable data for your project control and management of the implementation and execution of the project.

Summary

- *Develop the Work Breakdown Structure*
- *Use a multi-level approach*
- *Add additional activities if any identified*
- *Use a consistent approach*
- *Derive a Milestone Schedule with Must Dates*

Simple Scheduling

There are many instances where rigorous project planning analysis is not appropriate, justified or even possible, due to lack of accurate data. A "soft" project is a typical case where simple scheduling is sufficient in the early stages. Similarly, small, short-duration projects rarely justify using *Critical Path Methods* with rigorous analysis. Simple scheduling is the appropriate method to use. However, do not think that this eliminates all the key steps you have followed up to now. On the contrary, they are ALL still essential.

Simple scheduling, as the name implies, is a straightforward setting-out of all the project tasks in a logical graphic form that everyone can understand. This is usually done on a **Bar Chart**, a format first utilised by Henry Gantt in the early 1900s. It is a very convenient way of displaying all the activities and project tasks plotted against one or more parameters, although usually project time is the base

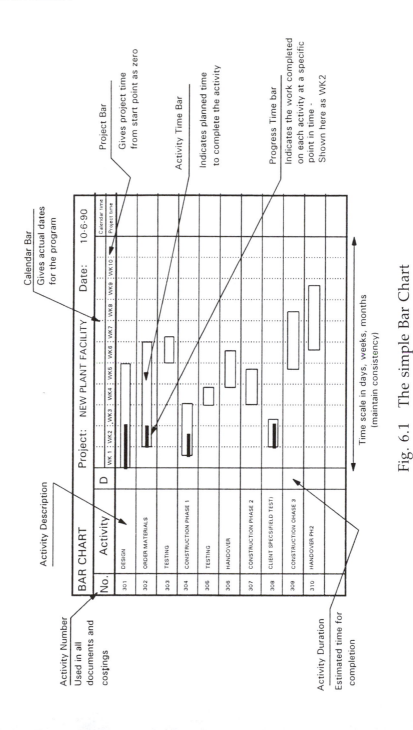

Fig. 6.1   The simple Bar Chart

parameter. Actual calendar time is usually also displayed in addition to the project duration. An example is shown in Fig. 6.1.

Additional information and key dates such as milestones, must dates, review meetings, progress status reports can also be displayed on the chart. Such charts can easily become very cluttered with data which is difficult to decipher, so keep words to a minimum. It is useful for repetitive data such as milestones, review meeting dates etc, to use a symbol – but do not forget to include a key to these at the bottom of the chart.

A primary advantage of this type of display of a schedule is the ease of updating and modification. Although simple to use and understand, it does have some shortcomings that are not always understood. Your ability to control and track a project using just the bar chart is therefore limited.

Limitations of the Bar Chart

However you try to arrange the activity list in a bar chart you cannot give an accurate representation of the relationships between the activities. Your efforts to derive the project logic are not totally wasted though, since this data can be utilised to partially show dependencies. This limitation restricts your ability to predict future activity priorities and their true inter-dependence.

The bar chart can only normally display the planned start of an activity based entirely on the activity durations and the project start date. If any activity starts late, the implications of this are not readily obvious. If this actually happens you will find it difficult to determine the consequent effects of such a slippage on other activities and on the time for completion of the project. For this reason, the bar chart can not really represent the true project status – activities that are behind schedule do not necessarily mean that the whole project is running late.

The last limitation of the chart is its inability to show uncertainty in performing any activity. You can obtain this data from rigorous analytical methods, but the bar chart is restricted to your initial estimates. If these are accurate then you will have no problems, but it would be a rare situation to find that all your estimates are accurate in practice. You cannot easily determine the consequences of an activity taking its shortest time to complete, or its longest time. Similarly, the most likely time or expected

time to complete cannot be evaluated in the context of the whole project.

These limitations do not mean that you cannot use the simple bar chart, since it is possible to overcome them to some extent. The most important shortcoming is the lack of obvious inter-dependency between activities and this can be partially resolved by rearranging the activity list. This allows you to display groups of related tasks together, clearly showing a sequence flow of work. However, attempts to display dependency between parts of each group with arrows can lead to a very confusing diagram.

Because of these limitations, the use of the bar chart for control can only be effective if you update it very regularly and re-issue copies to everyone involved. This requires a firm disciplined attitude towards using the bar chart alone, as there is always a tendency to put off re-issue until the next update!

Drawing Bar Charts

Before you start to use the bar chart you must decide on the format you are going to use and the exact information that is to be included on the chart. Once this standard is established, everyone knows what to expect and a consistent approach is beneficial for the team, the stakeholders and anyone else who has incidental involvement or interest in a project.

You must decide:

■ Chart size – A4 or A3 international standard – the latter is preferred for ease of drawing and clarity and you can easily reduce it to A4 on a photocopier

- Project information to include at the top:
  - project title and description
  - issue number and date
  - issued by (or drawn by) name and approved by name
  - cross-reference to other charts if applicable
  - units of project time: days, eight-hour days, weeks, months, etc
- System of coding of Key Stages and activities inside Key Stages
- The calendar period
- The accepted symbols to be used for:
  - activity duration as estimated
  - activity progress marked as completed
  - milestone points
  - progress review meetings
  - financial review points (if separate from milestones)
- Number of horizontal lines on chart – these must be sufficient to allow for additional activities to be added later and should be consistent with the requirement to keep the chart easy to read and uncluttered

These are the essential minima for drawing a bar chart. Remember also to include a key to any notations that are to be maintained as standard.

The practical drawing of the chart is best carried out by setting up a blank pro-forma incorporating the features and data you consider essential. In this way everyone can readily use the same format for the Key Stage plan as well as the exploded detail of any particular stage as appropriate. When you draw a chart, *always* use a soft pencil to draw in the activity duration bars! It saves paper and is easier to modify your master.

PROJECT PLANNING CHART

PROJECT:	PROJECT SCOR			DRAWN BY: TRD	APPROVED BY: GBW	SHEET 1 OF 1

KEY STAGE No: ALL

Line No	CODE	DESCRIPTION	Durn. day/wk/mth	RESOURCE NAME
1	A	Locate Building	5	
2	B	Plan layout	1	
3	C	Clean-up building	1	
4	D	Get all approvals	5	
5	K	Design IT&C equipt.	5	
6	P	Install IT&C equipt	2	
7	R	Install office equipt	1	
8	T	Test IT&C equipt	2	
9	L	Design fittings	3	
10	F	Quotes for mods	5	
11	M	Install mods	5	
12	N	Install fittings	2	
13	S	Install furniture	1	
14	U	Move staff	1	
15	V	Final testing	0.8	
16	W	Grand opening	0.2	
17	G	Furniture quotes	8	
18	H	Recruit staff	12	
19	E	Organise opening	1	
20		Progress meetings		
21				
22				

Project time: 1, 2, 3, 4, 5, 6, 7, 8, 9, 10, 11, 12, 13, 14, 15, 16, 17, 18, 19, 20, 21, 22, 23, 24, 25, 26, 27, 28

KEY:
Estimated Duration:
Completion to Issue Date:

Milestone Point: ◄
Progress Meeting: *
Finance Review: ■

Notes:

Date: 2-2-91
Original Issue Date: 2-2-91
Revision Number: 0

Fig. 6.2 Bar Chart for Project SCOR

> **STEP 12:**
>
> Prepare project schedule as a bar chart
> Design standard format for all charts
> Group related tasks together from Step 9
> Mark in agreed milestones
> Add agreed meetings schedule

The chart in Fig. 6.2 shows the Key Stages of Project SCOR arranged in groups that identify the project flow. It incorporates all the essential data and this format of chart is applicable to both Key Stage planning and exploded detail for each stage.

The resource names have not been completed because at this stage of planning you have not assigned responsibilities to anyone. In fact you may not yet know who is available to accept the additional responsibility of the work you need to have carried out as you implement the project execution. The next step is to assign responsibility for each activity and this may involve you in discussions with colleague managers to secure the type of resources you need. If you are using limited resources of different types and skills that are required to execute more than one activity in the project then it is valid to derive the **resource aggregation** through the project. This is discussed in more detail in Chapter 10.

Summary

- *Decide whether simple scheduling is adequate*
- *Design a standard format for Bar Charts*
- *Group related activities based on the logic*
- *Draw chart with activities in groups*
- *Mark in milestones, progress meetings etc*

The Critical Path Method

Simple scheduling provides you with a simple method of displaying all the work of the project. In a limited way it also allows the inter-relationships of the elements to be shown, but because it is essentially manually drawn it can be cumbersome to use. **Critical Path Methods** evolved to overcome these disadvantages and provide a procedure for managing projects that could be widely used as a common approach. The procedure was developed in the early 1960s to provide a graphical representation of the project based on a simple arithmetical process that identifies the relative importance of each element in the whole schedule. Two techniques have evolved and are in common use today:

■ The Critical Path Method – known as CPM

- The Programme Evaluation and Review Technique – known as PERT

This section confines itself to the application of CPM for the next step in planning your project. Many of the comments that follow apply to both techniques, although there are some important differences between them. The PERT technique is used by most project management software programmes and is particularly useful for large projects.

The CPM technique involves the graphical portrayal of the plan for the project as a structured diagram called a *network* which is based on the project logic. It provides you with a major advantage over simple scheduling. Because you can determine the underlying arithmetical relationship between the key stages of the project in terms of time, you are better equipped to make decisions in the control of the project. The technique can therefore be used for:

- Planning
- Scheduling
- Control

The technique still requires you to develop the basic project logic using methods you have used for the bar chart. To develop the schedule you use this information in a different way that is significantly more rigorous than the simple bar chart.

The procedures of CPM were developed initially in a technical environment. But this does not mean it can only be used for technical projects on a large scale. CPM can be used for any project, particularly where control is considered very important with strategic consequences. Once you are familiar with the procedures involved you will tend to use it always and if you are tempted to use a computer for project management then the critical path method gives you a consistent approach combined with rigorous recording of all relevant information as the project progresses.

Introducing CPM to your organisation

Like any management tool, CPM can be introduced in any organisation with care. If you are the first to adopt the technique for a project then take a few moments to consider the possible implications:

- CPM should not be treated as a mysterious wonder tool, known only to a select clique and presented as the panacea for all your planning problems. In fact, when not used correctly it can create more problems than it solves.
- CPM is not automatically a universal tool to use on all projects. Like any technique, there are limitations and occasions where it is not valid or appropriate to use it, eg for small, short-duration projects and continuous production.
- CPM should be adopted as an organisational standard, with firm guidelines as to when it is used/not used, and it should be understood and accepted by ALL levels of management. If necessary, managers and staff should receive appropriate training to appreciate the value of the technique and the role they have to take to ensure projects are successful.

The initial use of CPM can arouse considerable interest in your project with the resulting lack of interest in other less prestigious projects. If the going gets tough later this interest may turn into opposition and derision of the technique, which is unjustified. It is important that senior management demonstrate their enthusiasm and commitment and support to using and persisting with CPM for planning, scheduling and control of projects.

The elements of a network

In a network the project is displayed diagrammatically by *arrows* to represent the activities or tasks to be carried out and *circles* to represent the start and finish of such activities. Using just these two symbols a complete project network is developed. The network is drawn by combining these symbols together in a pattern to represent the logical dependencies derived with the *taskboarding technique* illustrated in Chapter 4. The elements of such a network are shown in Fig. 7.1 (A) and (B) with the accepted terminology for the components of the diagram. Because the arrows are used to represent the activities of the project these diagrams are sometimes called *Activity on Arrow* or "A on A" diagrams.

The circle is used to represent an event, that is a finite point in time which is initially the finish of an activity and simultaneously the start of the next activity. The diagram is telling you that the next activity cannot start under any circumstances until the previous activity is completely finished. The event is also known as a node, and there are three common types you will encounter in a network. These are shown in Fig. 7.1 (C) as:

- The straight *in line node*
- The *merge node* – where more than one activity is due to finish
- The *burst node* – where more than one activity is due to start

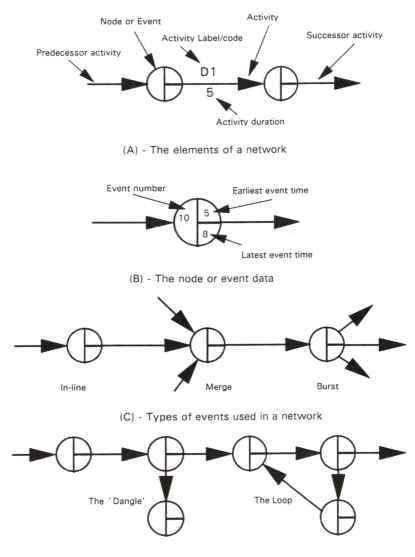

(A) - The elements of a network

(B) - The node or event data

(C) - Types of events used in a network

(D) - Possible errors in logic

Fig. 7.1   Graphic representation of Activity-on-Arrow
networks

Two possible errors of logic can appear sometimes, particularly in drawing complex networks. These are shown in Fig. 7.1 (D) as:

- The *loop* – where activities form an infinite loop due to the arrow been drawn "backwards"
- The *dangle* – where an activity arrow is drawn apparently leading to nowhere else in the network

This leads to some fundamental rules for the drawing of network diagrams:

- Although there is no time-scale normally associated with a network diagram, time is notionally presumed *always* to flow from *left to right* on the page
- *Tail* events must have a *lower* number then the corresponding *head event number* (see Fig. 7.2)
- Numbering of events should be from *left* to *right* on the drawing.
- Check the diagram for *continuity*, ensuring that there are no dangles and no loops

A checklist for drawing critical path networks is shown in Fig. 7.2.

When the drawing is completed you can carry out some further checks to ensure you have all the activities in the right place with respect to each other. At each event you can ask the fundamental questions:

- What has happened?
- What is happening now?
- What has to happen next?

This allows you to be quite sure that you are still satisfied with the initial dependencies you derived. It is also an opportunity, before you go any further, for you to review

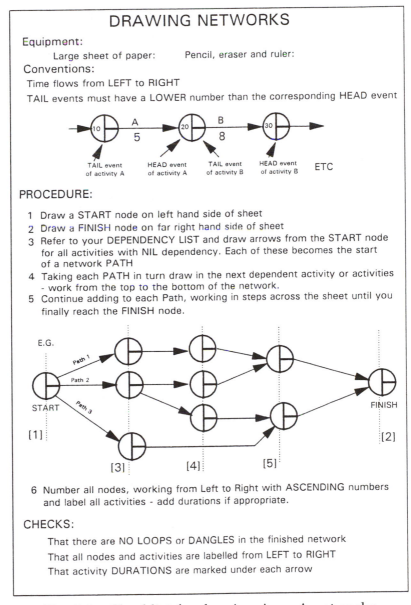

DRAWING NETWORKS

Equipment:

    Large sheet of paper: Pencil, eraser and ruler:

Conventions:

Time flows from LEFT to RIGHT

TAIL events must have a LOWER number than the corresponding HEAD event

TAIL event of activity A	HEAD event of activity A	TAIL event of activity B	HEAD event of activity B	ETC

PROCEDURE:

1 Draw a START node on left hand side of sheet
2 Draw a FINISH node on far right hand side of sheet
3 Refer to your DEPENDENCY LIST and draw arrows from the START node for all activities with NIL dependency. Each of these becomes the start of a network PATH
4 Taking each PATH in turn draw in the next dependent activity or activities - work from the top to the bottom of the network.
5 Continue adding to each Path, working in steps across the sheet until you finally reach the FINISH node.

E.G.

6 Number all nodes, working from Left to Right with ASCENDING numbers and label all activities - add durations if appropriate.

CHECKS:

    That there are NO LOOPS or DANGLES in the finished network

    That all nodes and activities are labelled from LEFT to RIGHT

    That activity DURATIONS are marked under each arrow

Fig. 7.2 Checklist for drawing A-on-A networks

your assessment of the key stages. If you find two or more key stages directly in series and lacking merge and burst nodes, ask if these can be combined into one key stage. Decide whether there is any point in separate identification – maybe they are executed by different departments which is a good reason to keep them separate. Any steps you can take to simplify a network diagram are worthy of consideration at this stage.

> ## STEP 13:
> *Draw the project network diagram*
> *Check network for continuity*
> *Number all nodes from left to right*
> *Check all activities are labelled*
> *Add activity durations under each arrow*

Finally, it is important to realise that except for very simple networks there is always more than one possible solution. You will find everyone has a different perception of the sequence in which work is performed and will derive slightly different dependencies and even different key stages.

This makes it yet more essential for you to involve your team and sometimes even the key stakeholders in this early part of planning. The final result is inevitably a compromise with which everyone can agree.

The network you have produced is effectively a statement of policy, but its real value so far has been to introduce you and your team to a disciplined approach to deriving your plan. Although you could also say the diagram itself is clear and free of ambiguity, it is not readily understood by everyone. It has some valuable, hidden secrets that can be very useful to you, both in further detailed planning and, later, project control.

The error of logic

Even the simplest logic can sometimes appear to let you down and this occasionally happens in a network diagram. You suddenly find you need to show that activities are dependent on each other when they are on different network paths. This is easily shown if you examine the network for Project SCOR shown in Fig. 7.3. You will observe that two activities are shown as dotted line arrows. These are called *dummy activities* because they have *zero durations* and are used to complete the logic.

You know from the dependency list that you have clearly identified that activity M (carry out modifications) is depend-

All durations in weeks.

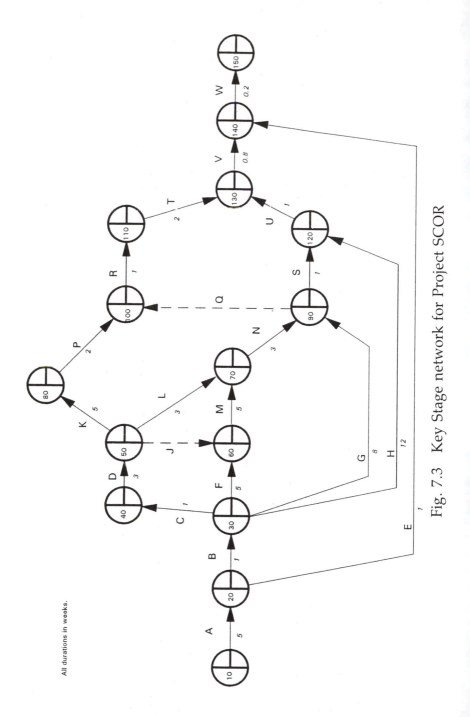

Fig. 7.3   Key Stage network for Project SCOR

ent on both activity D (get approvals) and activity F (collect quotes for modifications and decide). Because of the existence of a further activity L (design fixtures and fittings) with its dependencies, the only way the logic can be completed is to use the dummy – activity J. The dummy activity is treated like any other activity in the network. It is given a label and by convention has zero duration when the other activity's durations are assigned. It also creates a path through the network, just like any other activity. A second use of the dummy is shown as activity Q, which links completion of activity N (installation of fittings) and activity P (installation of IT&C system) before the start of office equipment installation in activity R.

It is almost inevitable that occasionally you will find it necessary to use a dummy activity and the only real problem often encountered is not the decision to use it, but its direction. The easiest way to ensure that you insert the dummy with the correct direction is to go back to your taskboard sheet where you showed dependency as arrows. Using this logic and remembering that the dependency flows along the dummy from the tail to the head (the reverse is illogical), then you should always get your dummy direction correct.

Analysing a network

Having completed the drawing of the network you are now keen to learn what you can get from it. As it stands it apparently has limited usefulness. The first step is to assign durations to every activity in the network. You may have done this already at the taskboarding stage of determining dependencies. If you didn't, then now you must put your estimating skills to the real test. With input from your team, and from anywhere else where time estimates can be obtained, you attempt to decide realistic times for each of your key stages shown as activities on the diagram. This may involve you in some detailed analysis of some of the key stages to determine reasonable estimates. For most small-to-medium projects it is often accepted that the activity durations are based on the time required for one person working full-time to complete the work (see Appendix Three). The purpose of analysing a network diagram is to determine the **total project time (TPT)** which is defined as:

the shortest time in which the project can be completed as determined by the sequence of activities in the network diagram which comprise the CRITICAL PATH.

The method of analysis requires you to carry out some simple arithmetical calculations to determine some specific characteristics of every activity in the network. These are:

- the *earliest starting time – EST*
- the *earliest finishing time – EFT*
- the *latest starting time – LST*
- the *latest finishing time – LFT*

Whereas these apply to every activity, each node or event has only *two times* associated with it:

- the *earliest event time – EET*
- the *latest event time – LET*

The EET is the earliest time that event can be reached with all the preceding activities completed, and must therefore be the earliest time any activity starting or emerging from the node can actually start. The LET is the latest time that

ANALYSING NETWORKS

REFERRING TO THE EXAMPLE NETWORK:

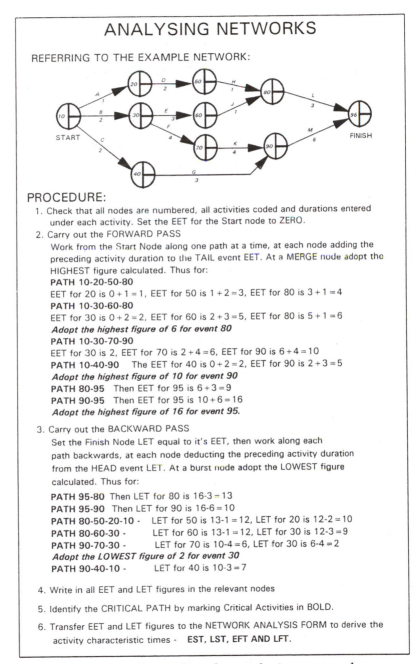

PROCEDURE:

1. Check that all nodes are numbered, all activities coded and durations entered under each activity. Set the EET for the Start node to ZERO.

2. Carry out the FORWARD PASS

   Work from the Start Node along one path at a time, at each node adding the preceding activity duration to the TAIL event EET. At a MERGE node adopt the HIGHEST figure calculated. Thus for:

   PATH 10-20-50-80
   EET for 20 is $0 + 1 = 1$, EET for 50 is $1 + 2 = 3$, EET for 80 is $3 + 1 = 4$
   PATH 10-30-60-80
   EET for 30 is $0 + 2 = 2$, EET for 60 is $2 + 3 = 5$, EET for 80 is $5 + 1 = 6$
   Adopt the highest figure of 6 for event 80
   PATH 10-30-70-90
   EET for 30 is 2, EET for 70 is $2 + 4 = 6$, EET for 90 is $6 + 4 = 10$
   PATH 10-40-90   The EET for 40 is $0 + 2 = 2$, EET for 90 is $2 + 3 = 5$
   Adopt the highest figure of 10 for event 90
   PATH 80-95   Then EET for 95 is $6 + 3 = 9$
   PATH 90-95   Then EET for 95 is $10 + 6 = 16$
   Adopt the highest figure of 16 for event 95.

3. Carry out the BACKWARD PASS

   Set the Finish Node LET equal to it's EET, then work along each path backwards, at each node deducting the preceding activity duration from the HEAD event LET. At a burst node adopt the LOWEST figure calculated. Thus for:

   PATH 95-80   Then LET for 80 is $16-3 = 13$
   PATH 95-90   Then LET for 90 is $16-6 = 10$
   PATH 80-50-20-10 -   LET for 50 is $13-1 = 12$, LET for 20 is $12-2 = 10$
   PATH 80-60-30 -   LET for 60 is $13-1 = 12$, LET for 30 is $12-3 = 9$
   PATH 90-70-30 -   LET for 70 is $10-4 = 6$, LET for 30 is $6-4 = 2$
   Adopt the LOWEST figure of 2 for event 30
   PATH 90-40-10 -   LET for 40 is $10-3 = 7$

4. Write in all EET and LET figures in the relevant nodes

5. Identify the CRITICAL PATH by marking Critical Activities in BOLD.

6. Transfer EET and LET figures to the NETWORK ANALYSIS FORM to derive the activity characteristic times - **EST, LST, EFT AND LFT.**

Fig. 7.4   Procedure for analysing networks

all activities entering that node can finish if succeeding activities are not going to be delayed.

The calculations are carried out by doing what is known as a *forward pass* through the network to determine the EET for each node. The process is then reversed to determine the LET for each node in a *backward pass*. By convention the EET and the LET of the last node in the network are made the same – on the basis that there is no spare time left at the end of the project. This time is then the *Total Project Time* or *TPT*. This is illustrated in an example in Fig. 7.4.

Identifying the critical path

It is possible to determine the critical path of small networks by inspection, an initial indication being the activities that lie on the network path through the nodes where the EET is equal to the LET. However, this is not an accurate test of criticality and the data must be extended to determine the true critical path. These event times you have calculated for each node effectively fix the boundaries between which activities are free to "move".

The lack of possible movement helps you to accurately identify the critical activities and the critical path. The event times are used to calculate the characteristic times for *each activity*:

- *the earliest start time* is given by the *EET* of the *tail node*
- *the earliest finish time* is given by adding the *duration* of the activity to the earliest start time (*EST*).
- *the latest finish time* is given by the *LET* of the *head node*
- *the earliest finish time* is given by subtracting the *duration* from the latest finish time (LFT**).**

It is usually relatively easy to write the data derived for event times on the network diagram as you analyse the diagram. With a little practice you can do the same for the activity times. However, if you have more than a few key stages in your project it is recommended that you use a standard format for identifying these times. This ensures that you do not clutter your drawing with notes and avoids possible errors. A suggested format is shown in Fig. 7.5.

Inspection of the tabulated data you have derived gives you much useful information about your project. Apart from identifying the characteristic times for each activity, it clearly identifies those activities with no capacity for movement. If you find for a particular activity that the *two start times* in Fig. 7.5 are identical, then the *two finish times* will also be identical. This is the true test of criticality, since

NETWORK ANALYSIS

PROJECT:					ANALYSIS BY: DATE:				
LINE	KEY STAGE / ACTIVITY				START TIMES		FINISH TIMES		TOTAL FLOAT
NO	Nodes	Code	Description	Duration Unit:	Earliest start	Latest start	Earliest finish	Latest finish	
	T	H							
1	2	3	4	5	6	7	8	9	10	11
1						|EETI	|LET -	|EET +	|LETI	
2							Durationl	Durationl	
3									
4									
5									
6									
7									
8									
9									

Fig. 7.5   Network analysis form

clearly the activity has no freedom for late start or delay. This condition is known as *zero float*.

If you now look for an activity where the two start times are different, then you will find the same arithmetical difference between the two finish times. If this test is not true and the difference of both pairs of data is not the same then you have made an error in calculation. This differential is the spare time in the activity, indicating that it can move within the fixed boundaries of time given by the "earliest" and "latest" condition. This spare time is known as the *total float* available for the activity.

If you mark all those activities with zero float you will identify the critical path, remembering that it:

- Starts at the very first node
- Is continuous through the network
- Ends at the very last node
- Identifies activities that must be carefully monitored

The analysis you have carried out has now identified the critical activities of your project and shows you where you have some spare time capacity. This information is invaluable when you come to assign people to the work that has to be executed.

STEP 14:

Analyse the network for criticality
  Carry out the forward and backward passes
  Determine the four activity characteristic times
  Identify total float available
  Establish the Critical Path

Obviously, knowing how much float you have in any part of a network is useful to your planning and control of the project. The total float you have identified is not necessarily all available to you to use in practice. You can find that moving an activity within the time boundaries may have an effect on other activities in the network. This could lead to previously non-critical activities suddenly becoming critical.

Using the format of Fig. 7.5, the full analysis of the network for Project SCOR is shown in Fig. 7.6. These data are frequently inserted in each node of the network to give a complete network diagram with the critical path identified as shown in Fig. 7.7.

Note the order of the activities on the analysis form. They are arranged in ascending order of the *head event number* and where there is more than one activity entering a node, then the listing changes to the order of ascending *tail event number* for that node only. The reason for adopting this simple rule is to assist you to draw the Gantt chart derived from your analytical data.

There are two other types of float which can be calculated, *independent float* which, as its name implies, can be used without affecting other activities: *free float* is float that can be used without affecting subsequent activities. For most projects it is sufficient to work with the total float and check the effects of moving an activity within your analysis.

NETWORK ANALYSIS

PROJECT: *SCOR*					ANALYSIS BY:	*BG*			
					DATE:	*03/09/91*			

LINE	Nodes		KEY STAGE / ACTIVITY			START TIMES		FINISH TIMES		TOTAL
NO	T	H	Code	Description	Duration Unit: *wks*	Earliest start	Latest start	Earliest finish	Latest finish	FLOAT
1	2	3	4	5	6	7	8	9	10	11
1	10	20	A	Locate Bldg	5	0	0	5	5	0
2	20	30	B	Plan layout	1	5	5	6	6	0
3	30	40	C	Clean bldg	1	6	6	7	7	0
4	40	50	D	Get approvals	5	7	7	12	12	0
5	30	60	F	Quotes for mods	5	6	7	11	12	1
6	50	60	J	DUMMY	0	12	12	12	12	0
7	50	70	L	Design fittings	3	12	14	15	17	2
8	60	70	M	Install mods	5	12	12	17	17	0
9	50	80	K	Design IT&C Equpt	5	12	13	17	18	1
10	30	90	G	Furniture quotes	8	6	12	14	20	6
11	70	90	N	Install fittings	3	17	17	20	20	0
12	80	100	P	Install IT&C Equpt	2	17	18	19	20	1
13	90	100	Q	DUMMY	0	20	20	20	20	0
14	100	110	R	Install office equpt	1	20	20	21	21	0
15	30	120	H	Recruit new staff	12	6	10	18	22	4
16	90	120	S	Install furniture	1	20	21	21	22	1
17	110	130	T	Test IT&C Equpt	2	21	21	23	23	0
18	120	130	U	Move staff	1	21	22	22	23	1
19	20	140	E	Plan opening	1	5	22.8	6	23.8	17.8
20	130	140	V	Final testing	0.8	23	23	23.8	23.8	0
21	140	150	W	Grand opening	0.2	23.8	23.8	24	24	0
22										
23										
24										
25										
26										
27										
28										
29										
30										

CRITICAL PATH IDENTIFIED AS:

EVENT PATH 10 - 20 - 30 - 40 - 50 - 60 - 70 -
90 - 100 - 110 - 130 - 140 - 150

TOTAL PROJECT TIME IS 24 WEEKS

Fig. 7.6 Network analysis for Project SCOR

All durations in weeks.

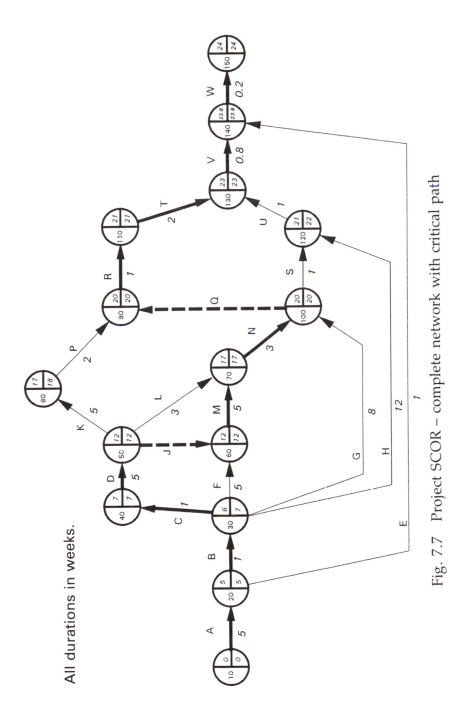

Fig. 7.7 Project SCOR – complete network with critical path

Summary

- *Draw the project network diagram*
- *Check that everyone agrees on the dependencies*
- *Agree duration of all activities*
- *Carry out the network analysis*
- *Identify critical activities and total float*

8

Using the Analytical Data

Now that you have a mass of data about your project you think "so what? What is the value of this information?" The purpose of the analysis is to establish:

- The critical activities – those to which you must give particular attention in monitoring
- The "float" or spare time available for all non-critical activities – time that you may need to use if some activities get delayed

This information is essential to you to maintain effective control of your project. However, it is easier to explain the implications of any actions you take if the data you have now derived is presented in the form of a Gantt Chart.

There are several ways to present the results from your

rigorous analysis of the network in a Gantt Chart, depending on personal preference. This chart may appear the same as a bar chart at first sight. But there are some important differences. Since the data are derived from a network where you have established the linkage between all the activities the bars are drawn on to the chart in the same order as listed in the analysis form, ie

- Activities are listed in *ascending order* of the *head event number*
- Merging activities are listed in *ascending order* of the *tail event number* for any particular node

The chart is then drawn by entering the time bar for each activity with a length equivalent to the duration. The start time used is the *earliest start time* for each activity.

Float time is also marked on the chart where this exists, and is usually shown by a different notation to the time bar for clarity. The critical activities have zero float and are easily distinguished, but they can be enhanced by using colour on the chart. When you have completed drawing the time bars you can add milestones and other information, such as progress meetings, as you did on a bar chart. A typical Gantt Chart for Project SCOR is shown in Fig. 8.1.

When the chart is drawn in this way it is possible to mark in the critical boundary line between the critical activities, shown as a broken line in Fig. 8.1. This represents the project limits and provides a quick view of the effects of delayed activities. Those activities that have float time available can move within the limits of the EST and the LFT like bars moving along slide rails. However, such movement may affect successor activities in the schedule. By marking the float time on the chart it is possible to

PROJECT PLANNING CHART

PROJECT: PROJECT SCOR

KEY STAGE No: ALL

DRAWN BY: TRD   **APPROVED BY:** GBW

SHEET *1* **OF** *1*

Date:

Project time: 1, 2, 3, 4, 5, 6, 7, 8, 9, 10, 11, 12, 13, 14, 15, 16, 17, 18, 19, 20, 21, 22, 23, 24, 25, 26, 27, 28

CRITICAL PATH LINE

Line No	CODE	DESCRIPTION	Durn. day/wk/mth	RESOURCE NAME
1	A	Locate Building	5	
2	B	Plan layout	1	
3	C	Clean-up building	1	
4	D	Get all approvals	5	
5	F	Quotes for mods	5	
6	L	Design fittings	3	
7	M	Install mods	5	
8	K	Design IT&C equipt.	5	
9	G	Furniture quotes	8	
10	N	Install fittings	3	
11	P	Install IT&C equipt	2	
12	R	Install office equipt	1	
13	H	Recruit staff	12	
14	S	Install furniture	1	
15	T	Test IT&C equipt	2	
16	U	Move staff	1	
17	E	Organise opening	1	
18	V	Final testing	0.8	
19	W	Grand opening	0.2	
20		Progress meetings		
21				
22				

KEY:
Estimated Duration: ▭
Completion to Issue Date: ▨

Milestone Point: ▲
Progress Meeting: *
Finance Review: ■
Total float: ●

Notes:

Date: 2-2-91

Original Issue Date: 2-2-91
Revision Number: 0

Fig. 8.1 Gantt Chart for Project SCOR

establish quickly the effects of this movement for any activity on later activities in the schedule. You may find on occasions that such movement causes a non-critical activity to turn suddenly critical by touching the boundary limit line. If an activity is delayed to the extent that it extends beyond the critical path line on the chart, then it could mean an extension to the total project time.

The Gantt Chart is one of the easiest ways of presenting the project plan in a graphical form that is readily understood by everyone. This and the dependency list from which it is derived are the two key documents from which you can generate the detailed planning you will do in the next phase of the process.

STEP 15:
Draw the KEY STAGE Gantt Chart based on EST data
Draw in the Critical Path boundary
Mark in all Total Float times
Use bullet points to mark in the milestones and
project Review Meetings

Up to this point you have been working with project time (in consistent units) and estimates of duration for each key stage or activity. These durations are normally based on the time required to complete all the tasks of the key stage or activity based on one person working full-time. So you have estimated on the basis of days or even hours of work, converted to normal working days. Alternatively, you may have decided to use direct hours of work as the basic unit for duration.

In reality the unit of person-days is unlikely to be a valid assumption. Since most projects today involve people working in a matrix environment it is inevitable that many of the team members do have other work to do, possibly on other live projects. Eventually you will determine the amount of time each has available for their part of the project. This will enable you to do a final assessment of resource availability for the project and attempt to balance this against the requirements under your plan. This could alter the appearance of the Gantt Chart, as some float may be needed on non-critical activities if you are short of resources at any time. However, you may make a decision to assign more resources to certain critical activities to shorten their durations. This will compress the network and reduce the total project time within certain limits.

These decisions have cost implications, so the Gantt Chart is a very convenient tool to examine the effects of trading off time against resources and costs. It is also very easy to-update the chart to show the consequences of making amendments forced on you by changing situations.

It is important to remember that planning is a re-iterative process, there is no absolutely right plan, only one that, based on the available information, appears to be the most appropriate! This re-iterative process really starts as you begin the process now of assigning resources to each key stage. On projects that will take several months to complete you may not be in a position to assign all resources at the outset, either due to unknown availability or lack of detailed planning at this point in time.

Before you can start to convert project time into real time that is calendar-based, you need to allocate responsibilities.

You will probably have a fairly clear idea of where you will do so, particularly when responsibilities cross functional barriers. This allocation does not reflect any changes to the durations of the key stages, but represents a decision about who is responsible for ensuring that the work of each key stage is executed on time. The time each individual will give to this work is a secondary decision derived by agreement, that is then inserted into the plan.

Summary

- *Ensure all activities are listed in correct order*
- *Draw the Gantt Chart*
- *Use Earliest Start Times for all activities*
- *Mark in Total Float on non-critical activities*
- *Mark in milestones and project meetings*

Allocating Responsibilities

The allocation of responsibilities needs to be recorded so that everyone involved with the project is quite clear on who will be doing what. The simplest way of presenting this information is to use a standard form of chart. This process is essential, irrespective of whether you have used the *simple scheduling method* or the *critical path method* to develop your plan up to this point.

The allocation of responsibilities is made after seeking agreement between you and the individual. If the individual is assigned full-time to the project as part of your team there should be little difficulty in getting agreement. However it is inevitable with most projects that part of the work will be the responsibility of another department. It is preferable if you can get someone in that department nominated as the **representative** to become a member of your team for as long as the work is being executed or even throughout the project.

The *representative* role is one of ensuring the work is actually carried out by someone in the department. That could mean actually doing all the work or assigning it to others. By allocating responsibility in this way you will ensure that day-to-day monitoring and control is carried out in the department where the work is in progress. This *representative* is often the line manager by choice, but it is not essential so long as the role receives functional line manager support. This ensures departmental commitment and attention given to priorities, so that your work gets done on time with the appropriate concern for performance and quality.

The standard chart can be conveniently used to record additional information such as:

- Who manages progress
- Who must be consulted if problems develop
- Who must be kept informed of progress
- Who is available for advice
- Who is referred to for key decisions

Others can also be listed on the chart when you design the format for your project. Some or all may be specific to a particular key stage or all the key stages. The **linear responsibility chart** is an important record document and not one just used at the planning stage. You must keep it under regular review and update it as required. People leave or move in the organisation and you must act promptly to re-assign responsibilities when this happens. A typical *Key Stages Responsibility Chart* is shown in Fig. 9.1.

LINEAR RESPONSIBILITY CHART   SHEET 1 OF 1

PROJECT: *PROJECT SCOR*   DRAWN BY: *TRD*   APPROVED BY: *GBW*

Line No	KEY STAGE No: ALL		Durn. day wk mth	RESPONSIBILIY NAME	Project Leader:							
	CODE	DESCRIPTION										
1	A	Locate Building	5									
2	B	Plan layout	1									
3	C	Clean-up building	1									
4	D	Get all approvals	5									
5	F	Quotes for mods	5									
6	L	Design fittings	3									
7	M	Install mods	5									
8	K	Design IT&C equipt.	5									
9	G	Furniture quotes	8									
10	N	Install fittings	3									
11	P	Install IT&C equipt	2									
12	R	Install office equipt	1									
13	H	Recruit staff	12									
14	S	Install furniture	1									
15	T	Test IT&C equipt	2									
16	U	Move staff	1									
17	E	Organise opening	1									
18	V	Final testing	0.8									
19	W	Grand opening	0.2									
20		Progress meetings										
21												
22												

NOTES:

KEY:
M - Manages progress
C - Must be consulted
I - Must be informed
A - Available for advice
D - Decision taker

NAME

Project Start Date:

Project Finish Date:

Fig. 9.1   Linear Responsibility Chart

In some projects you may have different types of resources employed which in turn may have cost implications on your budget. It is useful at this point to carry out a **resource aggregation** through the network or bar chart. Taking each key stage in turn and on each path, decide the different type of resources required for each activity. By adding these amounts cumulatively through the network/bar chart you will arrive at a complete aggregation for the project for each type of resource.

STEP 16:

Draw up the KEY STAGES Linear Responsibility Chart
Allocate Responsibility for each key stage
Identify interfaces with others
Carry out a Resource Aggregation for the project

You can use this data to display resource aggregation histograms directly below the corresponding part of the Gantt Chart/bar chart to give you a **resource type loading** for the project. An example of resource histograms is shown in Fig. 9.2, where you can see the effect of identifying the requirements or "loading" of three different resource types. Each activity is first analysed to identify the types of resource required, then the vertical totals for each unit of time are plotted as a vertical bar chart immediately under the corresponding point on the Gantt Chart/bar chart. Remember this is only a graphic display of resource types required, but it is the first step towards assigning the work in each resource type to specific individuals.

Resource aggregation is really a valuable step to carry out if you expect to need different resource types at different times in the project. As Fig. 9.2 shows, the resource type "C" is not required at certain times in this plan. Your initial observations, however, suggest that a problem of overloading could occur in week 5 with types "B" and "C". You may explore whether a "C" type resource could

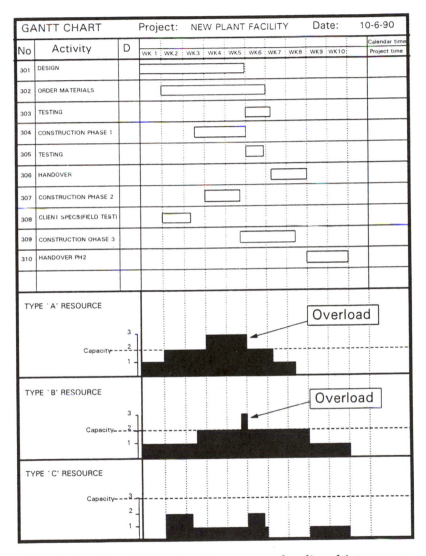

Fig. 9.2 A Gantt Chart with resource loading histograms

do some of the type "B" or "C" work with guidance or training to reduce the potential overload.

By comparing the loading with available capacity – the real time people actually can commit to the work of the project, you can determine if any real *overloading* occurs and exactly where it is in the plan. If you have used the rigorous approach with a *critical path analysis* you will find the float valuable because you can attempt to reduce the overload initially by sliding activities along the float lines within the EST and LFT limits you have calculated. If this does not overcome the problem, then you need to examine other options when you assign your resources. The simple bar chart does not readily identify "spare time" for any activity, so this process is one of trial and error to examine the consequences of moving an activity completion time. This is a limitation of simple scheduling and much time can be lost in assessing the effects of balancing resources against time and the effects on the total project time.

Summary

- *Identify responsibility for each key stage*
- *Assign to department representative if appropriate*
- *Draw up the Linear Responsibility Chart for the key stages*
- *Identify different resource types required*
- *Carry out a resource aggregation*

Allocating Resources to the Plan

If you are wondering why *allocating responsibilities* is treated as separate to *assigning resources* then refer back to Chapter 9. In this context, responsibility is allocated to the person whom you are asking to ensure the work gets done. If this individual is a departmental representative then he/she reports progress to you, but may assign part or all of the tasks involved to the appropriate people in the department. If everyone who is given a task to execute for your project attends a team meeting, you could sometimes find yourself addressing a rather large group!

By now you are anxious to start putting some real-time dates to your plan and this is only possible after allocating the resources. Only then will you know whether the activity durations you have used until now can actually be met in practice. In order to allocate resources to the plan you have to establish the availability of people and attempt to obtain a match between this and the plan requirements. This derivation of individual *loading* is essential to ensure no-one is overloaded with work beyond their normal capacity. Your estimates of duration have been made on the basis of work days (say one person working "n" hours per day, "d" days per week). Obviously an activity scheduled to take five days with one person working full-time will require more than one person if they can only devote half their time to the work. So each individual working on the project has to "contract" their calendar ahead to give you their availability or proportion of full capacity that can be used on your project work. To achieve this level of commitment for a long period of time forward is impossible due to the unforeseen events that you can expect to happen. Interruptions for unexpected crises are bound to interfere and you hope your inclusion of contingency in your estimates, combined with

NONSENSE! SHEENA'S TREMENDOUSLY EFFICIENT! SHE CAN COPE WITH A FEW EXTRAS!

available float where applicable, will minimise interference with your project progress.

For example, an individual works a five-day week, with 7.5 hours available each day. They have other responsibilities that occupy a minimum of three hours each day and they work on another project at the current time which is taking an average of one hour a day. This leaves them a maximum availability of 3.5 hours per day or 0.467 capacity for your work. By assessing capacity for each individual you can allocate the tasks to individuals to achieve full capacity for each day, ie:

- One person with a capacity of 0.467 plus
- One person with a capacity of 0.533, or two or more people whose total capacity adds up to 0.533

Alternatively, individual capacity can be examined on a weekly basis with available hours, attempting to match these against your needs within the time zone of the particular activity under consideration.

However, this assumes that the people all have the necessary skills for the job and that different skills are not required. Just like initial estimating, it is prudent in calculating available capacity to examine certain factors:

- Working efficiency – maximum real available hours
- Previous sickness and absenteeism record
- Current workload
- Holidays booked
- Any other constraints
- Cost and permits to work overtime

It is also important to decide the proportion of work of each key stage or activity that is assigned to specific skills. This is based on the **resource aggregation** you carried out earlier. Inevitably, the whole process is a balancing act between skills required, available capacity and plan needs. If you cannot satisfy the plan needs then you are faced with taking a decision. You have one of several options to consider (or a combination of these):

- Extend the activity duration beyond estimate into *float time*
- Seek additional skilled resources from somewhere
- Train additional resources in a crash programme
- Extend the *total project time*

Normally this process is ongoing throughout the project as you juggle your limited resources to maintain the project on the planned track. If your resources are charged to the project on a time basis you have an additional constraint to consider. Selecting a particular resource may be influenced by the cost which could force you to seek a less expensive option to maintain your budget and avoid overspending.

You do have a further option to consider, that of extending a non-critical activity beyond the boundary of the available float. The consequences of this decision need careful examination as there is a roll-on effect on successor activities that may extend the project time. But you may be able to reduce the duration of a later activity to recover the position, particularly if this is before the effect hits the start of a critical activity. Obviously, by definition any over-run of critical activities is serious and almost certain to extend the project time.

Your initial efforts are concentrated on attempting to adhere to the **key stage plan** as closely as possible and assign the work within the time constraints created by the analysis or Bar Chart. When you have achieved this it is valuable to record the agreements made with people in the form of a **Key Stage Assignment Chart** similar in format to the Linear Responsibility Chart. This will clearly show the actual assignments for everyone and there should be no misunderstandings amongst the team. An example of this chart is shown in Fig. 10.1, where the task assignments for a specific key stage are recorded. As you develop the

	KEY STAGE ASSIGNMENT CHART			SHEET OF					
PROJECT:				DRAWN BY:		APPROVED BY:			
Line No	KEY STAGE:			Responsible:		Project Leader:			Actual Finish Date:
	CODE	Start Date	Finish Date	TASK LIST					
1									
2									
3									
4									
5									
6									
7									
8									
9									
10									
11									
12									
13									
14									
15									
16									
17									
18									
19									
20									
21									
22									
NOTES:				KEY: M - Manages progress C - Must be consulted I - Must be informed A - Available for advice D - Decision taker		NAME			
Planned Start Date:									
Planned Finish Date:									

Fig. 10.1   Key Stage Assignment Chart

Work Breakdown Structure (WBS) to the level of detail appropriate for each key stage you can complete one of these charts. You will then accumulate a "family" of charts for the whole project (see Chapter 11).

With resource assignments agreed you can now insert real time dates into the Bar Chart or Gantt Chart with a reasonable level of confidence. You can adjust the lengths of activity bars on the chart to show any changes to actual durations now as a result of your resource allocations. Clearly you cannot carry out this process for the whole project at the outset, as people will not know their full commitments beyond the immediate future. This whole process is a continuing one as the project is implemented, planning the detail one to four weeks ahead and agreeing the resources needed.

STEP 17:
Draw up a Resource Assignment Chart
Identify and locate available resources
Agree available time for each resource
Resolve conflicts in the Bar Chart/Gantt Chart
Put Calendar dates into the Bar Chart/Gantt Chart

As with resource aggregation, the results of assigning work for all the key stages or activities can be presented graphically with a loading histogram, usually drawn under the corresponding parts of the Gantt Chart. This gives an immediate view of committed loading for each individual if you can produce a chart with all the histograms on the same sheet. You can also produce separate charts for each individual showing the agreed loading on your project.

It also has the advantage that it shows you the conflict situation where you have created an *overload* situation – committing more time to the project on a particular day or week than the individual has as available capacity. Loading histograms are usually drawn in two forms:

- All resources assigned per day
- Assignment by individual name

The use of computers has made this part of the planning process quicker and easier. Project management software programmes offer a wide range of options for examining resource calendars and resolving conflict situations that arise during planning and execution of the project. When an overload situation develops you can examine your options mentioned earlier to remove the conflict.

An alternative document to drawing histograms is the project calendar, one for each individual executing work on the project. This shows the available hours each day forward for one calendar month and really forms the basis of a "contract" between you and the individual and, if necessary, the functional line manager. This is specific to show time offered to your project, but other work is also sometimes listed as agreed commitments forward. As you work through the project assigning workloads you can derive a complete family of calendars for the project, including one for yourself.

Resource allocation is a time-consuming part of planning and really tests your skills as a negotiator and persuader to get what you want in the interests of the project. The process leads to agreements with individuals and line managers about assignments – effectively contracts. At intervals through the project, as more assignments are made, you issue the assignment charts with copies of the relevant Gantt Charts, calendars and any other information to the individuals as confirmation of their accepted commitments. There is really no excuse for anyone claiming they do not know what they are supposed to do, when or how.

The attention to detail required often leads to frustration and conflict with your own peer group as well as with other managers. But your perseverance will surely be rewarded with a project that stays on track and eventually reaches a successful outcome in accordance with all your plans.

Summary

- *Identify available capacity of individuals*
- *Locate and negotiate resource needs to satisfy plan requirements*
- *Record agreed commitments for the tasks in each key stage*
- *Draw up a Key Stage Assignment Chart for each key stage as details are developed*
- *Prepare resource histograms to confirm commitments and avoid overloading*

Layering the Plan

You have now reached the point where your plan based on the **key stages** is effectively complete. You have decided the logic of all events and developed the necessary documentation to illustrate this so that everyone involved understands what has to be done. The Bar Chart or Gantt chart is the principle guide map for the project and is supported by a list of responsibilities and even a list of work assignments for the initial key stages. The plan you have developed is described in the following documents:

- **The Objectives Statement**
- **The Scope of Work Statement**
- **The specification book**
- **The stakeholder list and valuations**
- **The logic diagram**
- **The Work Breakdown Structure**
- **The Milestone Schedule**
- **The KEY STAGE Bar Chart . . . . or**

- **The KEY STAGE Network Diagram and Gantt Chart**
- **The Linear Responsibility Chart**
- **The Work Assignment Chart**

For many small projects you think this is all you need to get the project moving into the execution phase. Before you action any work, however, there is something very important you must do – *get the project plans signed off* by the project sponsor. This will often require a project meeting with the sponsor and other key stakeholders to explain your plans and the decisions you have taken during planning, and to seek their acceptance and commitment. You have yet to establish the project costs based on your plan, but it is preferable to get the plan signed off before expending effort on a full costing.

Where each key stage only comprises a few tasks over a relatively short period of time you can agree the work with each responsible individual and monitor their progress. You know the amount of work involved in each key stage from the **Work Breakdown Structure** developed earlier. This needs to be reviewed with the team at this point to ensure that nothing has been omitted. You continue to carry out a review and update at regular intervals during execution of the work. However, there are two more tasks you have to carry out before you press the "GO" button.

Up until now money has been excluded from the process, but time is money, and you do need to consider the financial aspects of your plan and the decisions you have taken. Although your key stakeholders will be overjoyed with your attention to detail in planning the work, they will also be extremely interested (in some organisations) to know how much it is all going to cost. The **Project Budget** was probably set (in tablets of granite!) at the conception phase, but you must review this now and assess whether it is realistic and valid in the light of your planning decisions (see Chapter 12). •

You also need to establish some clear procedures to be adopted by the team for communicating progress, problems and status reports. This may be through existing organisational practices, but you decide how you want things done for your project, who gets what information, when and how it is distributed. Your role is to manage the project successfully in order achieve the objectives – not generate volumes of paper few people will read or possibly even understand! So you have a few more decisions to take (see Chapter 13.)

The planning flow diagram (Fig. 5.4) now takes the form shown in Fig. 11.1.

If there are many tasks in one or more of the key stages then you can now expand the project plan to include these in more detail, even planning to a third or lower level if necessary. This process of *layering the plan* ensures that you examine all the detail of the work involved and are better equipped to monitor progress.

If you know that some or all of your key stages comprises several tasks then expanding the plan to at least the second level is recommended. This will make the assignment of tasks easier to achieve and avoid any "fuzziness" about who is supposed to be doing what. If there is any scope for uncertainty in your plan then you can guarantee that it will be exploited by someone!

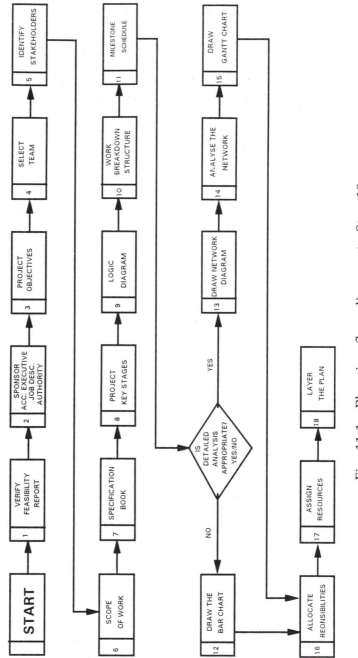

Fig. 11.1 Planning flow diagram to Step 18

Second level planning

The process of layering the plan involves *expanding* each *key stage* in turn to identify the detailed tasks to be completed. This requires you to return to *STEP 12* or *STEP 13*, depending whether you used simple scheduling or a critical path method. Each key stage is then examined separately for the intrinsic task content. This means producing a logic diagram for the key stage and inserting this data into the same processes you have carried out earlier.

If you are using *simple scheduling* then you can produce a separate bar chart for *each key stage* to give a complete family of charts that describes the plan for the whole project with all the detail.

If you are using the *critical path method* you take the logic diagram and the dependencies to produce a network diagram for the key stage. An example of this expansion for Project SCOR is shown in Fig. 11.2.

If this process is continued throughout the network a complete family of network diagrams is produced, one for each key stage. The benefit of this process is that you are really treating each key stage as a separate project or a *sub-project* of the main project. Each of these sub-projects has a specific critical path so that you can readily identify all the critical tasks that will need careful monitoring during execution. After analysis you can produce a corresponding family of Gantt Charts for the key stages of the project.

Responsibility allocation for each key stage has been made earlier. The person you have selected for this allocation can then be asked to carry out the task assignment for each Bar Chart or Gantt Chart produced. Your role here

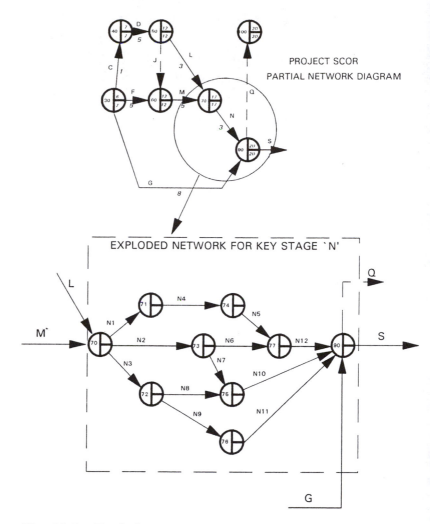

Fig. 11.2   Exploding a Key Stage of the Network Diagram

is to assist where necessary in obtaining the necessary resources, negotiating, persuading and occasionally using other methods to resolve any possible conflicts to obtain this resource. Having identified the detail of the key stage with its own internal critical links, the job of assigning the individual tasks is relatively easier. You can also ensure that the critical tasks are assigned to people with the appropriate skills, giving you the corresponding confidence level that they will be completed effectively on time.

STEP 18:

Layer the plan
　　Expand each KEY STAGE to show the detail
　　Derive the logic for each stage
　　Prepare Bar/Gantt Charts for the task list
　　Prepare Assignment Charts for each stage

At the end of this secondary planning process you have increased your project documentation to include:

- **The Logic Diagrams for each Key Stage**
- **The Bar Chart for each Key Stage . . . . or**
- **The Network diagram and Gantt Chart for each Key Stage**
- **The Work Assignment Charts for each Key Stage**

Of course this whole process can be reiterated for further levels of planning according to the size of the project. As stated earlier, the second or subsequent levels of planning do not need to be completed at the planning stage. In practice it is often impossible due to inadequate information, which is only generated in the early part of the project execution. As stated earlier, the next step is to produce the budget against the plan detail.

Summary

- *Get plans to date signed off*
- *Develop the detail of each key stage with the second level of the WBS*
- *Produce Bar/Gantt Charts for each key stage showing all the tasks to be executed*
- *Assign resources to the tasks in each stage*
- *Draw up Assignment Charts for each stage*

Establishing the Project Budget

Throughout the planning process so far, the budget has not been given any consideration. This is not to suggest that it is unimportant, but any attempt to update the budget as you plan is often difficult without sufficient detailed information. Many projects are conceived and then justified with a budget for senior management approval with minimal planning being done. The result is a continual potential source of conflict!

It is often considered that if a realistic budget is proposed, the project would never get approval, so costs are shaved to a minimal level. Then you have to spend more time justifying the overspends than monitoring and tracking the work. You can only produce the realistic budget after detailed planning, although previous project experience can give some useful "rule of thumb" indicators. The most significant cost for many projects is people, and this is where most estimates of cost go wrong due to over-optimism. The initial project budget that is established for financial approval should have some contingency or reserve, a figure that is usually an organisational standard based on a confidence level. It is important to establish the figure used – is it 5% or 35%? Whatever the figure, ensure that it is agreed with the key stakeholders.

Developing the project operating budget

Cash is a resource and can be treated in a similar way to the people resource, with histograms to illustrate cash used or committed on a project (see Chapter 9). This can be

aggregated for all costs or separated into the different types of costs associated with your project. The development of the project costs can only be achieved when the project activities have been identified with a high level of confidence. This presumes that the project has been clearly defined and the objectives agreed with the stakeholders. The cost of people's time is dependent on accurate estimating of the durations of the key stages or activities.

The **operating budget** is developed initially from the original project budget approved at the conceptual stage. Once the key stages of the project have been identified and the logic developed, the budget can be divided and apportioned to each of the stages. You base this division almost entirely on historical data and experience, knowing that as you layer the plan and develop the detail, you can progressively improve the accuracy of the budget data. The *operating budget* may include costs divided into the following types:

- *Capital costs* – usually associated with purchased items that can be depreciated
- *Revenue costs* – written off as running costs of the project, i.e. all except the people cost and contracts
- *People costs* – measured as time and converted to a "charge rate" for costing, often with "normal" working and "overtime" working rates
- *Contract costs* – costs derived from valid tenders and quotations that form the basis of an official order or contract.
- *Contingency or Reserve* – additional funding held separate to the main budget for unforeseen events and to cover the uncertainties in the original estimates.

Capital costs can be determined with reasonable accuracy from tenders and quotations and allowances made for inflationary effects. The revenue costs are often derived by a "rule of thumb" based on factors such as length of the project and the number of people involved. The people costs are attributed to the project in a variety of ways from zero through to accurate analysis, based on an individual's actual cost plus an overhead charge to cover fixed costs of the organisation. Because this is often the most significant cost in the project it is usually the one that leads to disagreement.

The contract costs are derived from tenders and quotations called for all external supplies. You must check the validity of all prices quoted and preferably request such prices to be given with sufficient validity to avoid having to go out for rebid, except where you need to modify the scope of supply. The project contingency is not normally an available fund. It is a reserve set aside by senior management with strict controls to ensure additional monies can be injected into the budget when problems occur. The release of any part of these funds is based on a full justification and is subject to (at least) approval by the project sponsor. Depending on the type and complexity of the project this fund may be a global sum or an amount phased through the budget. A phased contingency usually diminishes with project time and when not used in any period is considered lost to future access. This type of contingency is important if you are asked to produce a cash flow statement for the project.

Having identified the breakdown of the project budget into the key stages you can develop the **Key Stage Operating Budget**. This document is the basis of your future cost control reports to the key stakeholders. A typical format for the budget statement is shown in Fig. 12.1.

KEY STAGE OPERATING BUDGET

PROJECT:

Project Sponsor:
Project Leader:

Planned start date:
Planned finish date:

Account code:

Line No:	Key Stage Number	Description	Approved Budget (AP)	Approved Budget Variance	TOTAL (OP)	OPERATING BUDGET				
						Capital	Revenue	Contract	Labour	Direct hours
1										
2										
3										
4										
5										
6										
7										
8										
9										
10										

Approved Budget Variance (ABV) = (AP) - (OP)

Prepared By:

Date:

Approved By:

Date:

NOTE: All costs given in thousands of pounds

Fig. 12.1   Statement of the Key Stage Operating Budget

The *total operating budget* is derived from the *work breakdown structure*, initially focused on the key stages of the plan. You assess the costs for each key stage based on the level of detail developed and identified at the time. Since you have started to layer the plan the earlier key stages have been exploded to show the detailed tasks involved. You have negotiated work assignments and now know the resource costs associated with each part of the work to be completed. Developing these costs takes time, but is essential to your subsequent control of the project.

The cost of time is not always calculated as this requires all the individuals working on project tasks to record their committed time accurately for the accounting function to convert into financial data. If costs are not normally calculated in this way you should strive to get people to record the time in direct hours, ie time actually spent on project activities. The introduction of the need for timesheets is sometimes met with obstruction and even derision, but it is really essential if you are to control the costs of the project with any reasonable accuracy. Unfortunately, this need is not confined to your own immediate functional department. As you negotiate resources from other departments you will have to seek the support of functional managers for the process of keeping records of direct hours spent on your project. Clearly if you can persuade your project sponsor to direct this requirement to all managers, your control of the project is easier.

As you layer the plan progressively you can develop the operating budget statements for each key stage. In this way you derive a family of **Activity Operating Budget** statements for the whole project. This is particularly valuable for the larger projects where you are delegating part of the

ACTIVITY OPERATING BUDGET

Sheet   of

PROJECT:

Project Sponsor:
Project Leader:

Planned start date:
Planned finish date:

KEY STAGE NO:

Account code:
Responsible:

Line No:	Activity No:	Description	Assigned Resource	Approved Budget (AP)	Approved Budget Variance	TOTAL (OP)	OPERATING BUDGET				
							Capital	Revenue	Contract	Labour	Direct hours
1											
2											
3											
4											
5											
6											
7											
8											
9											
10											

KEY STAGE TOTALS

Approved budget:
Operating budget:
Variance

Prepared By:

Date:

Approved By:

Date:

Approved Budget Variance (ABV) = (AP) - (OP)

NOTE: All costs given in thousands of pounds

Fig. 12.2   Statement of the Activity Operating Budget

budgetary control to one of your team members, or where the work is totally executed in one department. A typical format for these statements is shown in Fig. 12.2.

As the detailed budget for each key stage is derived you must compare the totals with the project budget and analyse the variance. Clearly any negative deviation (indicating cost forecasts higher than the project budget) must be subject to close scrutiny and action planning to determine what action, if any, you can take to contain the situation. As a last resort you may have to justify the planned overspend and request the release of contingency funds if the expected situation becomes a reality.

STEP 19:

Derive the project Operating Budget
Divide Project Approved Budget within Key Stages
Derive costs for each Key Stage
Derive the Project Operating Budget
Seek approval of the Operating Budget

If the work of a key stage is totally carried out by another department then you can request the **departmental representative** who is a member of the project team to prepare the operating budget. You may have already asked this individual to prepare the work breakdown structure for the key stage, so preparing a budget is a natural extension of this planning activity. You must set down guidelines for the preparation of this budget. Be prepared to spend time negotiating with the representative and even the functional manager to get the budget agreed at a level acceptable to you in the context of the whole project. This builds a commitment to the work and its cost through the agreement achieved.

Pitfalls in costing

You may consider accurate costing of the project as a form of "mission impossible" and certainly the activity is full of potential difficulties and pitfalls. Some of the common pitfalls in costing the work include:

- Misinterpretation of the Scope of Work statement
- Poorly defined scope
- Lack of standards and specifications
- Poorly defined work schedules
- Omissions in the Work Breakdown Structure
- Poor assessment of individual skills and work rates
- Ignoring cost escalation and inflation effects
- Using estimates with no background supporting experience
- Ignoring forward increases in overhead costs
- Avoidance – especially bought-out services leading to guessing

Having reached this stage of planning you will probably be under considerable pressure to demonstrate that the project work is soon to commence. This leads to the costing exercise being given less effort than is really warranted and many of these pitfalls become easy traps for the unwary. Many of them do not show their consequences until later in the project and then the control system must respond with some prompt action to correct the situation.

Operating budget approval

As with each major step in the planning process it is important to seek the acceptance and approval of the operating budget by the key stakeholders before the project work is implemented. At this point you will be acutely aware of the accuracy of the project budget, particularly with respect to the early key stages that have been planned and costed in detail. Significant negative variances will now probably accumulate and increase with time as the project progresses. This point is often regarded as the primary *phase gate* of the project – an essential milestone point for release of funding. This is a means of controlling the release of funds for the project work to commence and clearly this can not occur until the operating budget is accepted and approved by the project sponsor. Major defects in the original project budget may demand a complete reappraisal of the objectives and scope of work. This phase gate is a significant decision point, since costs to date are only those associated with planning. A decision to abort the project is justifiable, or, with specific agreed actions the project continues with reinforced management commitment.

Summary

- *Apportion Approved Project Budget*
- *Estimate the costs for each key stage*
- *Derive the Project Operating Budget*
- *Identify cost variances from Approval Budget*
- *Identify potential contingency needs*
- *Derive Activity Operating Budgets for each key stage as detail is developed*

13

Preparing for Implementation

You have now completed the essential steps of planning with sufficient data to launch the project into action. As you have prepared the increasing detail of your plan you will have realised that planning is a dynamic process. There is a need to regularly review and re-iterate at any step in order to achieve what is apparently the best solution. Your objective is to arrive at decisions in the planning process that are acceptable to the team and the stakeholders and to build commitment for the execution phase of the project life cycle.

The need for re-iteration is most significantly apparent when the total project time you have derived is in conflict with the organisational requirements. It is a common situation where you have to compress your plans to achieve results sooner than your planning has initially shown to be possible. This causes you to repeat some of your work, firstly reviewing your estimates of duration for the key stages and then the tasks included in the *WBS*. You can then review your resource assignments to look for opportunities to speed up parts of the project. Of course this will lead you to re-negotiate the availability of existing and possibly additional resources. To do this forces you to make decisions and recommendations about the trade-offs between time, cost and performance in order to achieve the desired results. This process is not confined just to the planning phase and it is quite probable that you will be faced with similar decisions during execution.

A reduction in time may lead to increased project costs with no improved benefit in performance. In fact performance may also suffer as control procedures come under time pressure and cannot keep track of progress effectively. Similarly changes in performance may have hidden cost penalties or serious implications in the project schedule. Analysing the trade-offs requires you to assess the risks associated with the actions you decide to take. You must clearly identify the reasons for the trade-off, the assumptions you make and the actions you could take if problems develop later. However, when you complete the analysis and conclude with some decisions, you arrive at a plan that you can feel reasonably confident is based on careful planning, so that you can examine all the possible ways to achieve the objectives by means which are least detrimental in terms of time and cost.

Approving the plan

When you have derived the final plan, you need to collect all the essential documentation and charts together, along with any relevant supporting data sheets and information. This will include the second or lower level planning for the initial key stages and the project operating budget statements. The complete set of planning documents are then compiled in a suitable form for presentation to the key stakeholders for signing off as accepted and approved, even if various parts of the plan have had earlier approval.

This is best achieved by issuing the plan documents to the key stakeholders in advance of a project review meeting

where you describe the plan and allow the detail to be subject to scrutiny. Remember your purpose at this point is to create ownership, because you need the continuing support and commitment of these people. At the same time you must convince your stakeholders that you have derived a plan that is technically feasible and will achieve the project objectives approved earlier. If there are difficulties with locating sufficient resources, or with the project operating budget, then these conflicts must be resolved before the phase gate for project execution is opened. You should have enough background data to support your planning decisions and justify the actions you have taken to date.

STEP 20:
  Sign off the project base plan
    Finalise all project plan documents & budget statements
    Get plans accepted, approved and signed off
    Establish control system procedures & documentation

With project plans approved, the budget is released and you can move towards starting the project work. However, before you do this, take a little time to review the procedures you intend to use for controlling the project.

Establish project procedures

The **project control system** describes the essential elements of procedures you use for day-to-day operational control of the project. This system may already exist in the form of standard procedures and work practices. You must assess and decide if these existing procedures are acceptable to you or whether additional refinement is essential for your project.

Control is focused on the schedule and project cost estimates. As the project leader, control is your responsibility in order to create a climate which will enable the activity to be carried out effectively. Project control is made up of several key elements of communication:

- Monitoring – the surveillance process to find out what is happening
- An early warning system to identify hazards and problems
- Agreed methods of measurement of progress – particularly for the *critical success factors*
- Reporting procedures and associated documentation
- Recording of essential tracking data – costs and time
- Variance analysis procedure and reporting
- Planned project meetings at two levels:
    (1) With the project team
    (2) With key stakeholders

It may be appropriate to establish the elements of the control system before the plans are signed off by the key stakeholders. If project work using the techniques described here are relatively new to your organisation, then you must get support for the new procedures you plan to put in place. It is easy to get trapped into generating too much paper, but clearly you must have sufficient progress information recorded to enable you to control the project effectively.

There are numerous advantages for standardising many of the documents used in project control, just as is the case in the planning process. This reduces the time spent in administration by everyone involved since the consistent approach is easier to understand and breeds familiarity. This

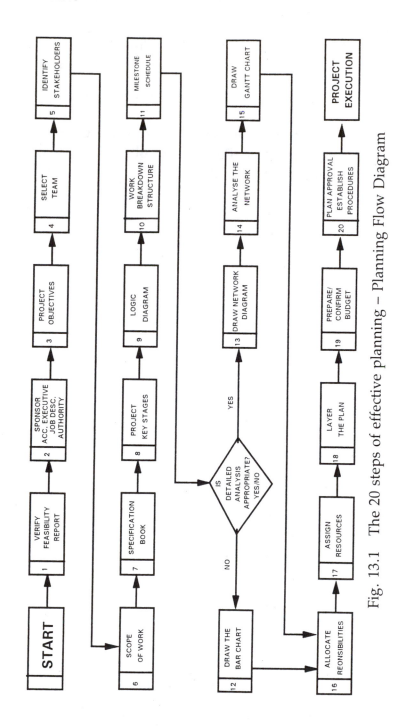

Fig. 13.1   The 20 steps of effective planning – Planning Flow Diagram

is discussed in more detail with the use of the documentation in *Implementing Projects* (see Appendix Five).

You have now completed the full planning methodology developed through from Step 1 to plan approval in Step 20, to give you **20 steps to effective planning of projects** as shown in Fig. 13.1. Occasionally you will pass by some steps or even change the sequence to suit your own needs, but with this model you can now approach your project planning in a more structured and logical manner.

A final word of caution

Planning your project so far is the easier part of your role as project leader. The costs to date are unlikely to be too significant, but the next step is going to prove whether your efforts have been worthwhile and effective. The full proof of planning is in the execution and you cannot relax your efforts to maintain control. Once the project work starts you have a complex role to fulfil, managing stakeholders, the project process and performance. If you have given the planning process sufficient time to develop the detail your efforts will be rewarded. Do not expect everything to go according to the plan. Unforeseen events are always going to occur which upset the plans and your success will be measured as much by results as by the perceived speed of response you give to problem solving and action planning needs as the project develops.

Success has been said to come from 1% luck and 99% hard work!

Summary

- *Collect together all project plan documents*
- *Issue plans to all key stakeholders*
- *Arrange a Project Review Meeting with all key stakeholders – including the team*
- *Present and describe plans and get stakeholder acceptance, approval and sign-off*
- *Establish the control system and all procedures and associated documentation*

Appendix 1
Setting Project
Objectives

Objectives are confused with aims and organisational mission statements. The latter are really statements which pull together the relationship between the resources, activities and customers of an organisation. The project objectives describe the position the organisation desires to achieve with respect to specific resources, activities and customers. These objectives must be:

- Specific – i.e. not broad or of a general nature
- Measurable – i.e. tangible and can be verified practically
- Achievable – i.e. attainable in the prevailing environment
- Realistic – i.e. possible with known available resources
- Timebound – i.e. given carefully designated timescales

You must verify that the objectives are also consistent with corporate strategy. Unfortunately, not all these characteristics are always immediately obvious in project objectives statements. Soft projects particularly have problems in establishing firm objectives until after all the possible alternatives are explored and management decisions taken. In these circumstances you must continually review the objectives, amending them as the work progresses.

The objectives statement

The objectives statement must have the characteristics listed and presented in a way which allows them to be easily understood by everybody involved with the project. It represents the framework for the scope of work to be carried out in order to achieve the desired results for the organisation. You need to derive a statement containing vital information which everybody accepts as valid and which receives stakeholder approval and ownership. There are five elements you should consider as a minimum:

■ **The perceived problem or need**
   The problem or need that has been identified as the source of the project is frequently based on perceived effects. It is always valid to examine this for underlying causes at an early stage to ensure that you clearly understand the problem you are attempting to resolve. Failure to do this could lead you to make erroneous decisions in the planning phase.

■ **The purpose of deriving a solution**
   You should make a simple statement of the organisational need to create a project for resolving the need

or problem. If there is no clear purpose then why are you doing it at all?

■ The benefits expected from deriving a solution

There are always benefits to be derived from any change, although not everyone is necessarily happy or agrees with that change. Yet the project is being established to satisfy strategic organisational needs, so the benefits can be identified. These must be accepted and agreed with stakeholders, who will usually have a significant input to their perceptions of potential benefits. Always ensure that benefits you list can be measured.

■ Definition of the results to be achieved

Having established purpose and benefits it should not be too difficult for you to define the more specific detail of the actual results to be achieved. These may be phased through the project, yielding cumulative benefits that you can identify. The results are the minimum acceptable for the project to be recognised as successful by the key stakeholders.

■ The deadlines for achieving the results

In the final part of the objectives statement you set out the timescales for the project, identifying the milestone dates for completion of each phase and the various stages in each phase. You must be realistic in setting these deadlines, making adequate provision for unforeseen events with reasonable contingencies. The milestone dates will be key progress reporting points in the project and are associated with key decisions and release of resources.

The **objectives statement** is the corner foundation stone supporting the fabric of your project. It is clearly relevant to give it adequate time and attention so as to ensure that you get the acceptance and commitment of the stakeholders to all the elements of the statement. Without this ownership your project is starting with a serious defect and the downstream consequences could be irreversible, with significant wastage of resources.

It is during the process of objectives-setting that covert or hidden agendas sometimes surface and you cannot afford to ignore them. Awareness allows you to be prepared for later situations when such hidden motives could be used to influence decisions in the planning, organisation or execution of the project. They can be used to your advantage at times, but equally they can be a source of blockage, creating barriers to progress and even on rare occasions outright sabotage! They may be personal to individuals or functional. In any organisation there is a tendency for departments to create a sub-culture of the organisational culture, influenced and directed by the manager. This is often the source of conflict across functional interfaces and you need to understand the differences that exist across the various interfaces you will need to influence at each phase of the project.

The statement is therefore your primary critical success factor and the key to setting the success criteria specific to your project. The **critical success factors** for your project are derived from the individual results or "deliverables" listed in the **objectives statement**.

A suggested format for the Objective Statement is given in Fig. A1.1.

STATEMENT OF OBJECTIVES

PROJECT TITLE:	JOB NUMBER:
	Sponsor:

Project Leader:	Accountable
Date Initiated:	Executive:

Problem / Need Statement:

Project Purpose:

Benefits expected:

Results to be achieved:

Project deadlines:	Milestone Dates:

Success Criteria:

Prepared By:	Checked By:	Approved By:
Date:	Date:	Date:

Fig. A1.1   Typical format of Statement of Objectives

Appendix 2
Brainstorming

The main purpose of brainstorming is to generate ideas which are normally based on experience, either from doing something in the past or from direct learning. Most people have a sub-conscious storage of a vast amount of information which is only called upon infrequently. In brainstorming you are trying to get at that data and find something useful to your project in there.

The technique has many variants and you are certain to use it many times during a project, from initially setting the objectives to problem-solving during the project. This is necessary in the execution phase to avoid unnecessary wastage of time and effort when using cause and effect analysis to clarify problems.

In the process you are attempting to take people away from logical vertical thinking to lateral thinking, where experience is used in a creative way to expose possible new ways of doing something. The best brainstorming results come from taking a logical, structured approach to the whole process. This means taking the process through a sequence of stages.

Stage One

State the purpose

Start by stating the obvious – what it is you are holding the brainstorming session for by having a written statement of the problem or need you are addressing. You may find it useful to prepare the session by putting this statement on a whiteboard or sheet of flip-chart paper on the wall to keep people's minds focused on the reason for their presence. Explain why you are using the group you have present and do not be confined to your team alone. It is often valuable to bring in one or two outsiders to keep ideas flowing, acting as catalysts with a few spontaneous wild ideas. Finally, check that everyone understands the statement you have presented, whether it is a problem or even the objectives of the project.

State Two

Set the ground rules

- Emphasise you are looking for QUANTITY not QUALITY
- Suspend all JUDGEMENT – ALL ideas are accepted and noted even apparently stupid or crazy ones

- Ensure there is no CRITICISM of anyone's idea, even through the use of body language
- Avoid DRY-OUT – keep things moving and stress it is important not to pause for reflection too much
- Stop questions about ideas from others
- Prevent explanation and clarification – pick it up later
- Note EVERYTHING down

The method of conducting the session varies considerably and if you have your own preferred way, then use it.

Stage Three

Conduct the session

The process is best carried out with someone acting as the leader to take the role of referee in case anyone breaks the rules. Although you want to promote free thinking, you must do this within a simple framework, otherwise the results will not meet your expectations. Some alternative ways are:

- *Taking turns* – arrange the group in a circle or "U" formation and go systematically around the group, asking each in turn for a contribution. If no idea is forthcoming allow a "pass". After two or three rounds allow the group to freewheel.
- *Singles* – allow each person present to work individually for the first five or ten minutes to write down as many ideas as possible. No talking is allowed in this opening part and this has the advantage that less dominant members of the group can prepare a contribution and not feel left out later. Follow this with the "Taking turns" method. If the group is large use small "buzz groups" of

two or three to work quietly for the same time before opening up the session.

■ *Freewheel* – usually best when some ideas already exist on the flip chart. Allow ideas to flow from anyone in the group in a random manner. This needs careful control by the referee to avoid one or two members of the group dominating the session.

In practice a combination of these methods is usually used according to the group size.

REMEMBER to note down EVERYTHING. A sure way to stop participation is to only write down what you think is relevant or important. If ideas seem to slow down or stop then DRY-OUT may have been reached. Do not attempt to push on, but take a break or adjourn for a while. Leave all your ideas generated on the flip-chart sheets available for people to look at – stick them up on the office wall! Another technique you can try at DRY-OUT is to open a dictionary at random and ask someone to select a word at random. Write this word down in large letters on a blank flip-chart sheet and ask everyone to concentrate on the word to see if it sparks off any fresh ideas. Giving the group a really wild idea which is obviously ridiculous can often have the same effect. It can lighten the atmosphere with the laughter it creates and frees people's minds from being channelled back into vertical thinking.

Stage Four

Evaluating the results

When you are satisfied that you have enough ideas you can start the process of evaluation. The group can carry out this process together to assemble all the ideas into "clusters" of related ideas or topics. If you have used the session to generate the list of probable tasks which are required to execute the project then these clusters will form the basis of the KEY STAGES. One way of proceeding is:

- Eliminate obvious "losers" – those which everyone agrees are inappropriate, unnecessary or ridiculous
- Sort ideas into groups and decide a label for each
- Check ideas for possible failure – try and determine if the idea is sound in principle and identify vulnerable aspects

If you are trying to solve a problem then you will reduce your list to a few options only using this technique. You can then home in on the most practicable option to apply to the problem.

Although you have eliminated ideas and reduced your list, it is prudent to retain ALL the data generated for reference later. You never know when it might be useful to refer to the lists again.

If it is project tasks you are grouping then you will reduce your list to the KEY STAGES of the project. The detail of the tasks in each group is not complete and almost certainly you will add to them later. For planning purposes you need to identify all the KEY STAGES first to derive the base plan. As you develop the plan into all its detail you can use the same brainstorming techniques to derive the full **Work Breakdown Structure.**

Appendix 3
Estimating

It is a common misunderstanding that CPM will give you accurate estimates and the project schedules will be correct through the rigorous analysis you have executed. Any rigorous analytical method is only as good as the data you provide for processing, so it is human error if estimates of time are subsequently found to be wrong. Unfortunately there is no easy way to derive accurate estimates for many project activities, particularly when a Key Stage could include a large number of individual tasks.

Who does the estimating?

The accuracy of time estimates for tasks and activities is related to who makes them. Some people have a talent for easily visualising what is involved in executing tasks and can give remarkably accurate estimates. You will soon get to know them by their reputation. Others appear to be quite hopeless at estimating. Although as a general rule the most knowledgeable person in the team or department should provide the estimates for any part of the work, past historical performance in estimating must be reviewed. The best estimates are usually derived by mutual agreement after discussion between the person who is most likely to be assigned the work and their immediate supervisor or manager. When it is impossible to identify the detail of the work involved it is necessary to use contingency, though it is important to ensure that any assumptions made at the time are clearly recorded.

Types of Estimates

Time estimates can be derived from four basic sources:

- **Historical data** – using data collected from past projects with similar activities. This can only be regarded as a guide since the data may be very outdated. In practice such data are often not accurately recorded for future use, so historical information becomes coloured with an element of hearsay!
- **Detailed analysis** – requires the full Work Breakdown Structure for the project to be available for accurate estimates to be assigned to every task. This is obviously important as the project implementation gets under way, but not always possible at the early stages of the project when initial time analysis needs to be carried out.
- **Guestimating** – inexplicably accurate estimating by the talented few who seem to have an intuitive ability to use some inspired guesswork to come up with accurate estimates.

- **Data records** – for certain types of projects, hard and reliable cost data are readily available from numerous sources. These are usually based on work study data collected over many projects with work study methods applied to the result and the people involved in producing the result. The data are often published in the form of Cost/Rate/Data books or even computerised.

Like planning, estimating is also a re-iterative process and the best results will only come from using as many sources as possible in deriving your project estimates. You will normally work with **activity duration**, ie the average time the activity should take, implying that the units are working days only with no account taken of the number of people assigned to any task.

Practical Steps

- Decide the number of working days available per week after allowing for holidays, training courses, sickness etc. This can often reduce the working week over several months to less than 4.0 days per week.
- Allow time within the estimates for management supervision and monitoring. This can vary from organisation to organisation but with small projects could rise to 15%.
- Take individual ability, experience and past performance into account as these factors influence time to execute a task.
- Initially, assume tasks are single-resourced – one person per task – as this makes estimation simpler. This ensures that the duration becomes the same as elapsed time for the task.
- Teamwork is important and each member of the team is

seeking personal development. When possible, involve the team in estimating discussions as this can lead to acceptance and commitment.

■ Allow a proportion of time in the estimates for unscheduled activities, particularly those created by functional requirements that are not project-related. Try to agree these figures with individuals and their line manager.

■ If regular project review meetings are essential, such as a crash programme in development, then allow time for these – they can't be "just squeezed in" somehow. Meeting schedules published well in advance the planning phase allow people to plan their time effectively.

■ Incorporate contingency, particularly at the primary planning level or in the Key Stage plan. Ensure contingency is not being accumulated blind at lower levels. As Project leader you must have a clear understanding where contingency exists in the plan and why it is there. This may involve you in **risk assessment** – identifying all the possible events that might happen which could jeopardise the project in some way. You can then plan what actions to take to avoid, minimise or limit the possible damages.

■ Major problems in estimating are encountered from time allowed for third party response to requests by the team. This can occur internally as well as externally and must be allowed for in your estimates. External stakeholders rarely admit to causing project delay, especially if they are funding the project, so an allowance for response time must be made based on experience.

■ Other factors that can affect estimates include:
  – statutory regulations and response
  – political dimension
  – economic situation (internal and external)

- weekend working and overtime hours (leading to extra holidays)

Research has shown that the use of rigorous analytical methods generally does not show any significant improvement in the quality of estimates as a direct consequence. However, it is clear that using these networking methods improves project scheduling and control through more efficient communication. It is this improvement in communication that directly contributes to increased performance in deriving accurate estimates. This is certain to improve your chance of completing the project successfully.

Appendix 4
Glossary of Project Management Terms

There is a considerable amount of jargon used by project managers today, enhanced by the rapid growth in the use of personal computers for planning and control of projects. The list gives some of the more common terms and their usual meaning.

Accountable Executive. The individual, usually a senior manager, who is held to account for the success of a project.
Action Cycle. The dynamic re-iterative process of actions that a leader follows to achieve results.
Activity. A clearly defined task with known duration: often

used to include a series of tasks which together complete a particular step or part of the work.

Activity on Arrow Diagram. A network diagram where all activities are represented by arrows and events represented by circles.

Activity on Node Diagram. A network diagram where all activities are represented by the node or event, usually as a box, and the arrows are used merely to show the logical flow of the project.

Arrow. The symbol by which an activity is represented in the Arrow Diagram.

Arrow Diagram. A diagrammatic statement of the complete project by means of arrows: also known as a **Network Diagram**.

Backward Pass. The procedure by which the latest event times or the finish and start times for the activities of a network are determined.

Bar Chart. A graphical presentation of the activities of a project derived from the project logic diagram, shown as a timed schedule.

Budget Variance. The analysed difference between the Approved Budget and the Operating Budget for the project, either as a project total or for each key stage.

Circle. The symbol used to represent an event, ie the start or finish of an activity.

Control System. The procedures established at the start of the project which provide the leader with the necessary data to compare planned status with the actual status at any instant in time, to identify variances and take corrective action.

CPM. Critical Path Method – a system where activities are represented by arrows on a diagram which can then be used for effective planning of the use of resources and subsequent control of the project.

Critical Path. The sequence of activities which determines the total time for the project. All activities on the critical path are known as **Critical Activities**.

Critical Success Factors. The factors that have a direct impact on the success of a project.

Dependency. The basic rule of logic governing network drawing – any activity which is dependent on another must be shown to emerge from the HEAD event of the activity on which it depends.

Dummy. A logical link, but which represents no specific operation (zero resources).

Duration. The estimated or actual time to complete an activity.

EET. The earliest event time – the earliest completion time for an event which does not effect the **Total Project Time**.

EFT. The earliest finish time of an activity without changing total time or the spare or float time.

Event. A point in the progress of the project after total completion of all preceding activities.

Float. Difference between the time necessary and the time available for an activity.

Forward Pass. The procedure for determining the earliest event times of a network.

Gantt Chart. A graphical method of showing a project schedule which shows project time, dates, all activities, resources and their relationships.

Hard Project. A project with clearly defined objectives and readily identifiable resource requirements from the outset.

Head Event. The event at the finish of an activity. The event then changes its nature and becomes the **Tail Event** for the succeeding activity.

Key Stage. A group of closely related activities that can be isolated together as a clear stage of the project which must be complete before proceeding to the next stage.

Let. The latest time by which an event can be achieved without affecting the Total Project Time from start to finish. **LFT.** The latest possible finish time without changing the total task or float times.

Milestone. Another name for an event, but usually reserved for a significant or major event in the project. Often used for identifying key progress reporting points.
Multi-level Planning. Planning the project at several levels of detail, starting with the key stages and then exploding each key stage to show all the associated activities. Where necessary, any activity is further exploded to show further detail of associated tasks at the next level down and so on.
Must Date. A planned date when an activity or group of activities must be complete under all circumstances.

Node. Another name for an event.

Precedence Diagram. A network where activity and dependency is shown by a box to represent the activity and an arrow to show the dependency link or logic. The arrows only serve to show the flow of the project between the nodes.
Predecessor. The activity immediately prior to an event.
Project Approved Budget. The budget approved at the conception of the project, based on outline plans only with contingency included.

Project Life-cycle. A systems approach to a project where the project is described as passing through four phases from conception to termination.

Project Operating Budget. The budget derived at operating level after detailed planning to first or preferably the second level is completed.

Resource. Anything other than time which is needed for carrying out an activity.

Resource Levelling. Utilisation of available float within a network to ensure that the resources required are appreciably constant.

Resource Smoothing. The scheduling of activities within the limits of their total floats to minimise fluctuations in resource requirements.

Semi-critical Path. That path which is next to the critical path when all paths are arranged in order of float.

Slack. Used to refer only to an event and is the latest date(time) minus the earliest date(time).

Soft Project. A project where the objectives are only broadly stated and the resources needed are unknown and flexible, the scope left open intentionally and deadlines not defined clearly.

Sponsor. The senior manager who takes ownership of the project on behalf of the organisation.

Stakeholder. Any individual who has an interest or stake in the project at any time during the project life-cycle.

Sub-critical Path. A path which is not critical.

Successor. The activity immediately following an event.

Tail Event. The event at the beginning of an activity.

Tail Slack. The slack possessed by an event at the tail of an activity.

Time Limited Scheduling. The scheduling of activities such that the specified project time is not exceeded using resources to a predetermined pattern.

Total Float. The total float possessed by an activity.

Tracking. The process of taking progress information gathered in a control system and inserting this into the original plan to show the actual status, ie the compliance or deviation from the planned status of the project at that point in time.

Work Breakdown Structure. The diagrammatic presentation of all the key stages and their associated activities arranged in a hierarchical format, showing each level of planning.

Bibliography

Effective Leadership
Adair, J. (1983. Gower Press)

Network Analysis for Planning and Scheduling
Battersby, A. (Macmillan, London) 3rd Edtion, 1978.

Advanced Project Management
Harrison, F. L. (Gower Press, Aldershot 1981)

Critical Path Analysis and Other Project Netwc Techniques
Lockyer, Keith (Pitman, London) 4th Edition 1984

CPM in Construction Management
O'Brien, J. J. (McGraw Hill, New York 1971)

Successful Project Management
Rosenau, M. D. Jr. (Van Nostrand Reinhold, New York

Project Cost Control Using Networks
Staffurth, C. (Heinemann, London) 2nd Edition, 1980

Planning by Network
Woodgate, H. S. (Business Books, London) 3rd Editic 1977

Implementing Projects
Young, T. L. (to be published 1993. The Industrial Socie London)

Leading Projects
Young, T. L. (The Industrial Society, London) 1993

British Standards Institution
BS 4335: 1972 Glossary of Terms used in project Netwo Techniques.
BS 6046: Parts 1, 2, 3, 4. Use of Network techniques project management.

The Manager as a Leader
The Industrial Society, London.